KU-442-764

THE RULES OF GOLF

By
TOM WATSON
With Frank Hannigan

Hodder & Stoughton
LONDON SYDNEY AUCKLAND

British Library Cataloguing in Publication Data
is available from the British Library

ISBN 0-340-58691-5

Copyright © 1992 by Golf Digest/Tennis, Inc.

First published in Great Britain 1985. This edition 1993.

All rights reserved. No part of this publication may be
reproduced or transmitted in any form or by any means,
electronic or mechanical, including photocopying, recording, or
any information storage and retrieval system, without either
prior permission in writing from the publisher or a licence
permitting restricted copying. In the United Kingdom such
licences are issued by the Copyright Licensing Agency, 90
Tottenham Court Road, London W1P 9HE.

This edition reproduced by arrangement with Golf Digest/
Tennis, Inc., A New York Times Company, and Pocket Books,
a division of Simon & Schuster

Published by Hodder and Stoughton,
a division of Hodder and Stoughton Ltd,
Mill Road, Dunton Green, Sevenoaks, Kent TN13 2YA
Editorial Office: 47 Bedford Square, London WC1B 3DP

Book design by Laura Hough
Photography by Steqhen Szurlej
Illustrations by Deborah Dutko
Cover photograph by Tom Meeks

Printed in Great Britain by
BPCC Hazells Ltd
Member of BPCC Ltd

CONTENTS

Playing the Ball

The Putting Green

Ball Moved, Deflected or Stopped

Relief Situations and Procedure

Other Forms of Play

Administration

FOREWORD

The United States Golf Association and the Royal and Ancient Golf Club of St. Andrews have carried out their customary quadrennial review of the Rules of Golf and have agreed upon certain amendments effective January 1, 1992.

The changes in the Rules are intended to provide clarification and are part of the continuing policy of simplification. The principal changes are summarized on pages 3 and 4.

The USGA and the R&A continue to enjoy the valuable assistance of golfing bodies throughout the world and will maintain their close liaison in all matters concerning the Rules and their interpretation. We would like to take this opportunity to express our sincere thanks to our respective Committees and to all those who have in so many ways helped us in our endeavors.

INTRODUCTION

This is the fourth edition of a book first published in 1980. It is published in conjunction with the revisions of the Rules of Golf for 1992.

The Rules are revised only every fourth year by the United States Golf Association and the Royal and Ancient Golf Club of St. Andrews, Scotland—the two organizations that write and interpret the Rules.

The USGA and R&A are uniquely influential and oddly devoid of actual power. They can only ordain that these Rules be used in their Championships, such as the U.S. and British Open Championships.

All of us who opt to use the Rules of Golf in other competitions and in everyday golf do so because we respect the USGA and R&A and because we recognize that uniformity in golf is eminently desirable. The game is more enjoyable if we all play the same game. There is a community of golf. It envelops the rawest of beginners, struggling to get around a course with a minimum of embarrassment but a maximum of hope, and those of us fortunate enough to play the game on the loftiest professional level. The Rules of Golf bind that community.

This edition, like its predecessors, is not aimed at any segment of the community of golfers. It assumes only the most basic understanding of golfer terminology. Beyond that point, I hope that it will be of help to golfers of all levels of experience and skills.

There was a time, actually not that long ago, when the Rules of Golf were regarded as the exclusive province of a handful of experts who spoke but rarely, and only obliquely.

That's changed. There has been an explosion in both interest in and understanding of the Rules marked by such developments as regular features on the Rules in magazines, by well-attended lectures and seminars sponsored by the USGA and the PGA of America, and—hopefully—by this book.

So much of the new understanding of the Rules was the result of the efforts of two men who passed away during 1991. Joe Dey was successively Executive Director of the USGA, Commissioner of the PGA Tour, and Captain of the R&A. He was also the great popularizer of the Rules of Golf. P.J. Boatwright succeeded Joe Dey as the USGA's great eminence on the subject. P.J. was so highly regarded that his very being seemed fused with the Rules.

My thanks again go to my friend C. A. (Tony) Wimpfheimer whose novel idea it was in 1979 that there should be such a book as this. He has fussed over and improved it constantly.

Over the years, the manuscript and illustrations have been inspected by many in the USGA family, all of whom have been inordinately helpful and patient. This time around it fell to Tom Meeks and Jeff Hall to keep us right down the middle.

ETIQUETTE

Prior to playing a stroke or making a practice swing, the player should ensure that no one is standing close by or in a position to be hit by the club, the ball or any stones, pebbles, twigs or the like which may be moved by the stroke or swing.

Consideration for Other Players

The player who has the honor should be allowed to play before his opponent or fellow-competitor tees his ball.

No one should move, talk or stand close to or directly behind the ball or the hole when a player is addressing the ball or making a stroke.

In the interest of all, players should play without delay.

No player should play until the players in front are out of range.

Players searching for a ball should signal the players behind them to pass as soon as it becomes apparent that the ball will not easily be found. They should not search for five minutes before doing so. They should not continue play until the players following them have passed and are out of range.

When the play of a hole has been completed, players should immediately leave the putting green.

In the absence of special rules, two-ball matches should have precedence over and be entitled to pass any three- or four-ball match, which should invite them through.

A single player has no standing and should give way to a match of any kind.

Any match playing a whole round is entitled to pass a match playing a shorter round.

If a match fails to keep its place on the course and loses more than one clear hole on the players in front, it should invite the match following to pass.

Holes in Bunkers

Before leaving a bunker, a player should carefully fill up and smooth over all holes and footprints made by him.

Replace Divots; Repair Ball Marks and Damage by Spikes

Through the green, a player should ensure that any turf cut or displaced by him is replaced at once and pressed down and that any damage to the putting green made by a ball is carefully repaired. Damage to the putting green caused by golf shoe spikes should be repaired *on completion of the hole.*

Damage to Greens—Flagsticks, Bags, etc.

Players should ensure that, when putting down bags or the flagstick, no damage is done to the putting green and that neither they nor their caddies damage the hole by standing close to it, in handling the flagstick or in removing the ball from the hole. The flagstick should be properly replaced in the hole before the players leave the putting green. Players should not damage the putting green by leaning on their putters, particularly when removing the ball from the hole.

3

Golf Carts

Local notices regulating the movement of golf carts should be strictly observed.

Damage through Practice Swings

In taking practice swings, players should avoid causing damage to the course, particularly the tees, by removing divots.

DEFINITIONS

If you skip this section on Definitions and jump right to the Rules, you're making a mistake. You can't learn the Rules without understanding the Definitions which exist because many of the key words and special terms in the Rules cry out for clarification.

Golfers tend to resort to the Rules only when they have a problem and are in a hurry for an answer. They'll run into a phrase such as "through the green" and draw a blank—because "through the green" is misused commonly by television commentators who mistakenly apply the words to balls hit *beyond* the green.

Or take the rudimentary "stroke." It's a word that applies only to the *forward* movement of a club.

So here come the Definitions, punctuated by occasional comments, which, if you'll excuse the pun, are inserted to define the Definitions.

Addressing the Ball

A player has "addressed the ball" when he has taken his *stance* and has also grounded his club, except that in a *hazard* a player has addressed the ball when he has taken his stance.

It's important to know that a ball has not been addressed outside a hazard until the club has been grounded. That means a player is off the hook if the ball is precariously perched and rolls, providing the player has not grounded the club or done anything else to cause the ball to move.

Advice

"Advice" is any counsel or suggestion which could influence a player in determining his play, the choice of a club or the method of making a *stroke.*

Information on the Rules or on matters of public information, such as the position of hazards or the flagstick on the putting green, is not advice.

The second paragraph means it's not asking for advice to say "Where's the hole?" But watch out. There are some tricky Decisions on "advice," summarized in the text following Rule 8.

Ball Deemed to Move

See "Move or Moved."

Ball Holed

See "Holed."

Ball Lost

See "Lost Ball."

Ball in Play

A ball is "in play" as soon as the player has made a *stroke* on the *teeing ground*. It remains in play until holed out, except when it is *lost, out of bounds* or lifted, or another ball has been substituted under an applicable Rule, whether or not such Rule permits substitution; a ball so substituted becomes the ball in play.

Rules of Golf experts seem constantly to answer a question with another question: "Was the ball in play?" because the ruling so often turns on the answer. So it's a vital Definition that says a ball is "in play" as soon as the player has made a stroke on the teeing ground. It remains in play until

7

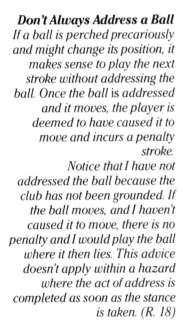

Don't Always Address a Ball
*If a ball is perched precariously
and might change its position, it
makes sense to play the next
stroke without addressing the
ball. Once the ball is addressed
and it moves, the player is
deemed to have caused it to
move and incurs a penalty
stroke.*
*Notice that I have not
addressed the ball because the
club has not been grounded. If
the ball moves, and I haven't
caused it to move, there is no
penalty and I would play the ball
where it then lies. This advice
doesn't apply within a hazard
where the act of address is
completed as soon as the stance
is taken. (R. 18)*

holed out, except when it is lost, out of bounds or lifted, or another ball
has been substituted under an applicable Rule.

There can only be one ball "in play" for one player at any time. Thus, if
a player's ball heads in the direction of a water hazard and the player
drops and plays another ball, the second ball is then "in play." Should the
player find and play the original ball, whether in a water hazard or not,
he's played a "wrong ball."

Bunker

A "bunker" is a *hazard* consisting of a prepared area of ground,
often a hollow, from which turf or soil has been removed and
replaced with sand or the like. Grass-covered ground bordering or

within a bunker is not part of the bunker. The margin of a bunker extends vertically downwards, but not upwards.

If you insist on calling it a "sand trap," you've fallen into the trap of substituting common usage for correct language. The phrase "sand trap" is not in the Rules. It's a bunker.

Caddie

A "caddie" is one who carries or handles a player's clubs during play and otherwise assists him in accordance with the Rules. When one caddie is employed by more than one player, he is always deemed to be the caddie of the player whose ball is involved, and *equipment* carried by him is deemed to be that player's equipment, except when the caddie acts upon specific directions of another player, in which case he is considered to be that other player's caddie.

Since caddies commonly carry two bags, it's necessary to sort out who is penalized when a caddie breaks a Rule. Example: When a caddie, indicating the line of putt for one of his players, touches A's line with a flagstick, A is penalized. Partner B is not.

Casual Water

"Casual water" is any temporary accumulation of water on the *course* which is visible before or after the player takes his *stance* and is not in a *water hazard.* Snow and natural ice, other than frost, are either casual water or *loose impediments,* at the option of the player. Manufactured ice is an *obstruction.* Dew and frost are not casual water.

For the benefit of us hardy Northeners who venture out on the course during winter, a 1992 clarification has been made: Frost, like dew, is not casual water.

Committee

The "Committee" is the committee in charge of the competition or, if the matter does not arise in a competition, the committee in charge of the *course.*

In everyday golf, the Committee is not likely to be on the site. The golf professional is usually authorized to act for the Committee.

Competitor

A "competitor" is a player in a stroke competition. A "fellow-competitor" is any person with whom the competitor plays. Neither is *partner* of the other. In stroke play foursome and four-ball competitions, where the context so admits, the word "competitor" or "fellow-competitor" includes his partner.

"Competitor" is an old-fashioned word with a nice ring to it. The people with whom you are playing in stroke play are "fellow-competitors." They are not your "partners" or, worse yet, "playing partners." Calling them such is inaccurate and can cause Rules problems since "partner" suggests a team relationship. You are not in business with a fellow-competitor.

Course

The "course" is the whole area within which play is permitted. See Rule 33-2.

Equipment

"Equipment" is anything used, worn or carried by or for the player except any ball he has played at the hole being played and any small object, such as a coin or a tee, when used to mark the position of a ball or the extent of an area in which a ball is to be dropped. Equipment includes a golf cart, whether or not motorized. If such a cart is shared by two or more players, the cart and everything in it are deemed to be the equipment of the player whose ball is involved except that, when the cart is being moved by one of the players sharing it, the cart and everything in it are deemed to be that player's equipment.

Note: A ball played at the hole being played is equipment when it has been lifted and not put back into play.

An amendment to the Rules for 1992 illustrates the way the code is handled by the USGA and R&A. The Definition now clarifies the status of golf carts. It says that a cart shared by two players and everything in it are deemed to be the equipment of the player whose ball is involved, but with a vital disclaimer: When the cart is in motion, the cart and everything in it are deemed to be the driver's equipment.

A word to the wise: When you are searching for your ball in a cart, let the other person in the cart become the designated driver because if the cart rolls over your ball neither of you is penalized provided the driver is not your partner. By the way, that's not a Rules change per se for 1992, but what used to be found only in a Decision has now been incorporated into the body of Definitions.

Fellow-Competitor

See "Competitor."

Flagstick

The "flagstick" is a movable straight indicator, with or without bunting or other material attached, centered in the hole to show its position. It shall be circular in cross-section.

I wonder why we find it so cute to call it a "pin" when the right word— "flagstick"—is more evocative and says so clearly what the thing is.

Forecaddie

A "forecaddie" is one who is employed by the Committee to indicate to players the position of balls during play. He is an *outside agency.*

Ground Under Repair

"Ground under repair" is any portion of the *course* so marked by order of the Committee or so declared by its authorized representative. It includes material piled for removal and a hole made by a greenkeeper, even if not so marked. Stakes and lines defining ground under repair are in such ground. The margin of ground under repair extends vertically downwards, but not upwards.

Note 1: Grass cuttings and other material left on the course which have been abandoned and are not intended to be removed are not ground under repair unless so marked.

When Is a Ball in Ground Under Repair?

This ball is in an area marked ground under repair because it touches the line. I'd be entitled to take relief even if the ball was outside the area, because my stance caused me to stand on the line or within the marked ground. (R. 25)

Grass in a Bunker

The Rules allow you to ground your club in a grassy area within a bunker. Grass-covered ground within a bunker is not considered part of the hazard. By the way, these are the famous "church pews" within a bunker at the Oakmont Country Club near Pittsburgh. (Def.— Bunker)

11

Note 2: The Committee may make a Local Rule prohibiting play from ground under repair.

Ground under repair is customarily defined by white lines. When the ball touches the line, it is in ground under repair. Here's a Decision on ground under repair:

● Is a rut or groove made by a maintenance vehicle considered a hole made by a greenkeeper and thus qualifies as ground under repair?

Answer: No, but a player whose ball is in a deep rut would be justified in asking the Committee to declare the ruts to be ground under repair, and the Committee would be justified in doing so.

Hazards

A "hazard" is any *bunker* or *water hazard*.

Hole

The "hole" shall be 4¼ inches (108mm) in diameter and at least 4 inches (100mm) deep. If a lining is used, it shall be sunk at least 1 inch (25mm) below the *putting green* surface unless the nature of the soil makes it impracticable to do so; its outer diameter shall not exceed 4¼ inches (108mm).

Holed

A ball is "holed" when it is at rest within the circumference of the hole and all of it is below the level of the lip of the hole.

Honor

The side entitled to play first from the *teeing ground* is said to have the "honor."

Lateral Water Hazard

A "lateral water hazard" is a *water hazard* or that part of a water hazard so situated that it is not possible or is deemed by the Committee to be impracticable to drop a ball behind the water hazard in accordance with Rule 26-1b.

That part of a water hazard to be played as a lateral water hazard should be distinctively marked.

Note: *Lateral water hazards should be defined by red stakes or lines.*

We need a better name to describe this kind of hazard in the future because, as the definition says, a "lateral water hazard" need not run laterally, or parallel, to the line of play. It's up to the Committee to make the distinction, and the Committee is supposed to decide on the basis of whether it's practicable to drop behind the hazard and keep the spot where the ball last crossed the margin between the player and the hole. If not, the hazard should be identified as "lateral," giving the golfer the two extra options expressed in Rule 26-1c.

Line of Play

The "line of play" is the direction which the player wishes his ball to take after a stroke, plus a reasonable distance on either side of the intended direction. The line of play extends vertically upwards from the ground, but does not extend beyond the hole.

Line of Putt

The "line of putt" is the line which the player wishes his ball to take after a stroke on the *putting green*. Except with respect to

Rule 16-1e, the line of putt includes a reasonable distance on either side of the intended line. The line of putt does not extend beyond the hole.

"Loose impediments" are natural objects such as stones, leaves, twigs, branches and the like, dung, worms and insects and casts or heaps made by them, provided they are not fixed or growing, are not solidly embedded and do not adhere to the ball.

    Sand and loose soil are loose impediments on the *putting green,* but not elsewhere.

    Snow and natural ice, other than frost, are either *casual water* or loose impediments, at the option of the player. Manufactured ice is an *obstruction.*

    Dew and frost are not loose impediments.

Rules experts are in love with the "half-eaten pear" Decision. It deals with the arcane matter as to whether a half-eaten pear in a bunker is a natural object (and thus a loose impediment that can't be moved in a bunker) or an artificial object, since it's been altered by man. It was

Loose Impediments

Sand Can't Always Be Removed
Sand has been splashed from a bunker onto both the putting green and the apron just off the green. Both areas are on my line to the hole and might affect the roll. Nevertheless, the sand off the green is not *a loose impediment and may not be moved; the sand on the green is a loose impediment and may be removed. (R. 23)*

decided that a pear is a pear is a pear, whether chomped on or not, and thus retains its status as a loose impediment.

That is not to say that some loose impediments can't be transformed into obstructions. For instance, a log that's been split, painted, and joined to legs has been changed into a bench—an artificial object.

Lost Ball

A ball is "lost" if:

a. It is not found or identified as his by the player within five minutes after the player's side or his or their caddies have begun to search for it; or

b. The player has put another ball into play under the Rules, even though he may not have searched for the original ball; or

c. The player has played any stroke with a *provisional ball* from the place where the original ball is likely to be or from a point nearer the hole than that place, whereupon the provisional ball becomes the *ball in play.*

Time spent in playing a *wrong ball* is not counted in the five-minute period allowed for search.

This Definition is bound to raise corollary questions. You'll find many questions and answers as to when a ball is lost or not in the text following Rule 27.

Marker

A "marker" is one who is appointed by the Committee to record a *competitor's* score in stroke play. He may be a *fellow-competitor.* He is not a *referee.*

Matches

See "Sides and Matches."

Move or Moved

A ball is deemed to have "moved" if it leaves its position and comes to rest in any other place.

It follows then that a ball has not moved, and there's no penalty involved, if the ball only jiggles, or oscillates, when it's touched by a clubface as the ball is being addressed.

Observer

An "observer" is one who is appointed by the Committee to assist a *referee* to decide questions of fact and to report to him any breach of a Rule. An observer should not attend the flagstick, stand at or mark the position of the hole, or lift the ball or mark its position.

Obstructions

An "obstruction" is anything artificial, including the artificial surfaces and sides of roads and paths and manufactured ice, except:

a. Objects defining *out of bounds,* such as walls, fences, stakes and railings;

b. Any part of an immovable artificial object which is out of bounds; and

c. Any construction declared by the Committee to be an integral part of the course.

No Relief from Boundary Fence or Stakes

Even though they are artificial objects, out of bounds stakes and fences and their posts are not obstructions. Moreover, boundary stakes, posts and fences are regarded as "things fixed" and may not be moved. In this situation, I can either try an awkward stroke, without moving the stake, or declare the ball unplayable. (R. 28)

The Committee has the latitude to say, in effect, that you don't get relief from an artificial object called an "integral part of the course." The best example in all of golf occurs on the 17th hole, The Road Hole, of the Old Course at St. Andrews, Scotland. If there were free relief given from balls on the road, the hole, as good a par-4 hole as there is anywhere, would be spoiled.

Out of Bounds

"Out of bounds" is ground on which play is prohibited.

When out of bounds is defined by reference to stakes or a fence or as being beyond stakes or a fence, the out of bounds line is determined by the nearest inside points of the stakes or fence posts at ground level excluding angled supports.

When out of bounds is defined by a line on the ground, the line itself is out of bounds.

The out of bounds line extends vertically upwards and downwards.

A ball is out of bounds when all of it lies out of bounds.

A player may stand out of bounds to play a ball lying within bounds.

In Bounds or Out of Bounds

The out-of-bounds line is determined by the inside points of stakes or fence posts at ground level. A ball is out of bounds only when all *of it lies out of bounds. Rules of Golf officials sometimes decide close calls by stretching a string from stake to stake. The ball at left is out of bounds; the ball at right is in bounds. (R. 27)*

Outside Agency An "outside agency" is any agency not part of the match or, in stroke play, not part of the competitor's side, and includes a referee, a marker, an observer or a forecaddie. Neither wind nor water is an outside agency.

Golf balls are often deflected by alien objects and creatures such as dogs, spectators and trash containers. They are all "outside agencies."

Partner A "partner" is a player associated with another player on the same side. In a threesome, foursome, best-ball or four-ball match, where the context so admits, the word "player" includes his partner or partners.

A "penalty stroke" is one added to the score of a player or *side* under certain Rules. In a threesome or foursome, penalty strokes do not affect the order of play.

Penalty Stroke

A "provisional ball" is a ball played under Rule 27-2 for a ball which may be *lost* outside a *water hazard* or may be *out of bounds.*

Provisional Ball

Two key points:
1. You can play a provisional ball in both stroke play and match play.
2. You cannot play a provisional ball only for the reason that your ball may have entered a water hazard.
And make the distinction between a provisional ball, which is available in order to save time, and a "second ball"—an option available only in stroke play—when you are in doubt as to the Rules of the proper procedure.

The "putting green" is all ground of the hole being played which is specially prepared for putting or otherwise defined as such by the Committee. A ball is on the putting green when any part of it touches the putting green.

Putting Green

You'll not find the word "apron" or "collar" in the Rules. We take them to mean the strips of low-cut turf just *off* greens.

A "referee" is one who is appointed by the Committee to accompany players to decide questions of fact and apply the Rules of Golf. He shall act on any breach of a Rule which he observes or is reported to him.
A referee should not attend the flagstick, stand at or mark the position of the hole, or lift the ball or mark its position.

Referee

Few golfers ever have the chance to play with a referee accompanying them, a formality that puts the game on a most lofty plane. There's no reason why referees can't be assigned to club events, but they better know what they're doing. The USGA offers the definitive work on the subject in a low-cost booklet, "How to Conduct a Competition." (Write to USGA, Far Hills, N.J. 07931)

A "rub of the green" occurs when a ball in motion is accidentally deflected or stopped by any *outside agency* (see Rule 19-1).

Rub of the Green

The term "Rule" includes Local Rules made by the Committee under Rule 33-8a.

Rule

SIDE: A player, or two or more players who are *partners.*
SINGLE: A match in which one plays against another.
THREESOME: A match in which one plays against two, and each side plays one ball.
FOURSOME: A match in which two play against two, and each side plays one ball.

Sides and Matches

17

THREE-BALL: A match play competition in which three play against one another, each playing his own ball. Each player is playing two distinct matches.

BEST-BALL: A match in which one plays against the better ball of two or the best ball of three players.

FOUR-BALL: A match in which two play their better ball against the better ball of two other players.

Again, be aware of usage. A "threesome" and a "foursome" properly describe forms of competition—not three or four people who happen to be playing together.

Stance

Taking the "stance" consists in a player placing his feet in position for and preparatory to making a *stroke*.

Stipulated Round

The "stipulated round" consists of playing the holes of the course in their correct sequence unless otherwise authorized by the Committee. The number of holes in a stipulated round is 18 unless a smaller number is authorized by the Committee. As to extension of stipulated round in match play, see Rule 2-3.

The classic dispute on a stipulated round dealt with a match in which two players inadvertently skipped two holes. They did not realize the omission until the results of the match were posted. One player had won 1 up. The Committee sent the two players back out to play the two missing holes and, naturally, the player who was 1 down won both holes, changing the result.

Did the Committee do the right thing?

Answer: The Committee's decision is final (see Rule 34-3). However, the Committee should *not* have directed that the two omitted holes be played belatedly. The result of the match should have been allowed to stand as originally posted—see Rule 2-5. Had the players agreed to play less than the stipulated round, both would have been subject to disqualification—see Rule 1-3.

Stroke

A "stroke" is the forward movement of the club made with the intention of fairly striking at and moving the ball, but if a player checks his downswing voluntarily before the clubhead reaches the ball he is deemed not to have made the stroke.

Here's what some Decisions have to say about strokes:

• A player disgustedly raps his ball off the green after missing a short putt. Was that a stroke? No, but the player incurs a one-stroke penalty and must replace the ball.

• A player plays a stroke at his ball but then learns that the ball was out of bounds. Answer: He played a wrong ball since a ball out of bounds is no longer in play.

• The weaker partner in a foursomes event purposely "whiffed" a ball rather than attempt to carry it over a water hazard. Answer: Nice try, but that was not a stroke since it was made without the attempt to hit the ball. As soon as the stronger partner played after the "whiff," the team played out of turn and incurred the appropriate penalty under Rule 29.

The Teeing Ground
The teeing ground is a rectangular area two club-lengths in depth. You can tee your ball anywhere in that rectangle. You are not required to stand within it. I've chosen to stand outside the teeing ground in the bottom picture because I feel that setup makes it easier to stay out of the trouble that lurks on the left side of the hole. (Def.—Teeing Ground)

Teeing Ground

The "teeing ground" is the starting place for the hole to be played. It is a rectangular area two club-lengths in depth, the front and the sides of which are defined by the outside limits of two tee markers. A ball is outside the teeing ground when all of it lies outside the teeing ground.

19

Here we run into "club-lengths" for the first time. You'll find it throughout the Rules. It's a term of measurement used rather than a specific distance; e.g., "six feet," because golfers don't carry tape measures. Any club is acceptable and, obviously, a driver is the best candidate since it will make for the biggest rectangular area. Come to think of it, that contemporary horror known as the "long putter" also qualifies.

Through the Green

"Through the green" is the whole area of the *course* except:
a. The *teeing ground* and *putting green* of the hole being played; and
b. All *hazards* on the course.

Here we find the three words that encompass most of the course but not all of it. Excluded are the tee of the hole being played, the putting green of the hole being played, and any hazard on the course. Everything else is "through the green." These distinctions are often critical. For instance, if your ball is just off the green and there's casual water between you and the hole, you get no relief—that is, you may not move the ball because it's "through the green." But if the ball is on the putting green, a special kind of relief is available under Rule 25-1.

Water Hazard

A "water hazard" is any sea, lake, pond, river, ditch, surface drainage ditch or other open water course (whether or not containing water) and anything of a similar nature.
All ground or water within the margin of a water hazard is part of the water hazard. The margin of a water hazard extends vertically upwards and downwards. Stakes and lines defining the margins of water hazards are in the hazards.
Note: *Water hazards (other than* lateral water hazards) *should be defined by yellow stakes or lines.*

There are only two kinds of water hazards. One, the more common, is often referred to (but not in the Rules) as a "regular" water hazard. The other is a "lateral water hazard." Knowing which is which matters because the relief procedures are different and more generous if the hazard is lateral.

Wrong Ball

A "wrong ball" is any ball other than:
a. The *ball in play,*
b. A *provisional ball* or
c. In stroke play, a second ball played under Rule 3-3 or Rule 20-7b.
Note: *Ball in play includes a ball substituted for the ball in play when the player is proceeding under an applicable Rule which does not permit substitution.*

THE RULES
OF PLAY

THE GAME

RULE 1

THE GAME

The Game of Golf consists in playing a ball from the <u>teeing ground</u> into the hole by a <u>stroke</u> or successive strokes in accordance with the Rules.

1-1.
General

No player or caddie shall take any action to influence the position or the movement of a ball except in accordance with the Rules.
PENALTY FOR BREACH OF RULE 1-2:
Match play — Loss of hole; Stroke play — Two strokes.
Note: *In the case of a serious breach of Rule 1-2, the Committee may impose a penalty of disqualification.*

1-2.
Exerting Influence on Ball

Players shall not agree to exclude the operation of any Rule or to waive any penalty incurred.
PENALTY FOR BREACH OF RULE 1-3:
Match play — Disqualification of both sides; Stroke play — Disqualification of competitors concerned.
(Agreeing to play out of turn in stroke play — see Rule 10-2c.)

1-3.
Agreement to Waive Rules

If any point in dispute is not covered by the Rules, the decision shall be made in accordance with equity.

1-4.
Points Not Covered by Rules

1-1. General

The Rules of Golf begin with a concise definition of the game itself. One sentence of 27 words does the job.

Right here, at the beginning, start to notice the key words carried over from the Definitions. The rules-makers go to the trouble of underlining every such word in the text. Begin to get comfortable with the precise language used throughout the Rules. There are no fewer than five checkpoints in this sentence of 27 words.

• Playing "a" ball means playing *one* ball. You may not change to a shiny new ball once you've cleared a water hazard and landed safely on a putting green.

• The "teeing ground," according to the Definition, is "the starting place for the hole to be played," and its dimensions are specific.

• "Into the hole" is a warning that if you fail to hole out in stroke play, a form of play which does not allow for a conceded stroke, you haven't played the game. The result must be disqualification.

• "By successive strokes" calls for an understanding of a stroke which the Definition says "is the forward movement of the club made with the intention of fairly striking at and moving the ball." (Richard Peters came to play in the first U.S. Amateur Championship in 1895 intending to putt with a billiard cue. There is no such thing as a stroke made with a billiard cue, because a billiard cue is not a club. Peters, denied his pet, lost his first round match by 5 and 4.)

• "In accordance with the Rules" is what this book is about. In order to understand and enjoy the game you should know the Rules.

1-2. Exerting Influence on Ball

Examples of what Rule 1-2 means (taking "any action to influence the position or the movement of a ball") are found in Decisions.

• A player purposely steps on and damages (or improves) his opponent's line of putt. Violation!

• On a windswept coast of Wales a player cleverly placed his bag parallel to the line of a short putt to shield the line of putt from the wind. Violation!

• During a California Amateur Championship at stroke play a competitor holed out and then repaired spike marks on the line of a fellow competitor. Nice guy, but violation! If the player whose line was affected had sanctioned the improvement, he too should be penalized, but under Rule 13-2.

• A player's ball overhangs the edge of a hole. He jumps as high as he can, three feet from the ball, jarring the earth. The ball falls in. Violation!

• As an act of sportsmanship, a player removes a loose impediment—a stone or leaf—adjacent to an opponent's ball in a bunker. No matter what the motive, the player lost the hole by taking an action to influence the position or lie of the opponent's ball.

1-3. Agreement to Waive Rules

Rule 1-3 expresses the principle that golf is meant to be the same game for everyone with the same code of Rules and the same set of penalties. It becomes a different game, for instance, when opponents agree in advance they'll concede every putt "within the leather." They've made an agreement to ignore Rule 1-1, and both should be DQ'd. Concessions must be dealt with on a case-by-case basis.

Because Rule 1-3 is vital to the integrity of the game, interpretations have been consistently strict. Key decisions:

• In a match, a player discovers she has 15 clubs in her bag. The opponent says, "Forget it. Just take one club out of play. No penalty." The player says "Thanks," and they play on. Unfortunately, there is not only a penalty, but it's golf's version of the death penalty. Both players are dis-qualified for agreeing to waive a Rule.

• Opponents agree that they'll waive the prohibition against repairing damage caused by spikes. When the Committee learns what they've done, both are disqualified even though their actions did not affect the play of anyone else.

• A player drew a blank and failed to hole a tiny putt in a stroke- play round. Her marker (another competitor in the same group) observed the violation but signed the scorecard anyway, treating the un-holed putt as if it were conceded in a match. Both players were aware of the violation.

Answer: Both the player and the marker are disqualified.

1-4. Points Not Covered by Rules

No set of Rules can cover every conceivable occurrence and it's there-fore necessary to rule occasionally "in equity," but never when an incident is covered by a Rule or a Decision. Here's a sampling of "equity" decisions:

• A player took a hefty swipe at a ball on a wet embankment. The ball stuck to the face of the club.

Answer: The player should drop the ball as near as possible to the spot where the ball was when the ball stuck to it. There's no penalty, but the stroke already made counts.

• A ball came to rest so near a bird's nest that it could not be played without damaging the nest. The decision-makers, in what some might call an uncharacteristic burst of humanity, say the ball can be dropped away from the nest without penalty.

• In a decision much loved by the USGA, a player stepped into a bunker and was shocked to see a rattlesnake near her ball. Her opponent report-edly said, "Play it."

Answer: It's not reasonable to expect a player to play from such a dangerous situation. The player is allowed to play without penalty in the hazard, or in a similar nearby hazard, where there is no danger. The same applies to bees and wasps. Indeed, a similar ruling was made for players in a bunker infested by yellow jackets in a U.S. Amateur Championship. And, to emphasize how humane the rules-makers are, the original ball need not be retrieved.

On the other hand, Brett Upper asked for a drop out of a patch of poison ivy in the 1991 World Series of Golf and was properly told, "Play it." So while danger may lie in the eye of the beholder, it's up to the Committee in charge to split the hairs of an "equity" decision.

RULE 2

MATCH PLAY

In match play the game is played by holes.

Except as otherwise provided in the Rules, a hole is won by the side which holes its ball in the fewer strokes. In a handicap match the lower net score wins the hole.

The reckoning of holes is kept by the terms: so many "holes up" or "all square," and so many "to play."

2-1.
Winner of Hole;
Reckoning of Holes

25

A side is "dormie" when it is as many holes up as there are holes remaining to be played.

2-2.
Halved Hole

A hole is halved if each side holes out in the same number of strokes.

When a player has holed out and his opponent has been left with a stroke for the half, if the player thereafter incurs a penalty, the hole is halved.

2-3.
Winner of Match

A match (which consists of a stipulated round, unless otherwise decreed by the Committee) is won by the side which is leading by a number of holes greater than the number of holes remaining to be played.

The Committee may, for the purpose of settling a tie, extend the stipulated round to as many holes as are required for a match to be won.

2-4.
Concession of Next Stroke, Hole or Match

When the opponent's ball is at rest or is deemed to be at rest under Rule 16-2, the player may concede the opponent to have holed out with his next stroke and the ball may be removed by either side with a club or otherwise.

A player may concede a hole or a match at any time prior to the conclusion of the hole or the match.

Concession of a stroke, hole or match may not be declined or withdrawn.

2-5.
Claims

In match play, if a doubt or dispute arises between the players and no duly authorized representative of the Committee is available within a reasonable time, the players shall continue the match without delay. Any claim, if it is to be considered by the Committee, must be made before any player in the match plays from the next teeing ground or, in the case of the last hole of the match, before all players in the match leave the putting green.

No later claim shall be considered unless it is based on facts previously unknown to the player making the claim and the player making the claim had been given wrong information (Rules 6-2a and 9) by an opponent. In any case, no later claim shall be considered after the result of the match has been officially announced, unless the Committee is satisfied that the opponent knew he was giving wrong information.

2-6.
General Penalty

The penalty for a breach of a Rule in match play is loss of hole except when otherwise provided.

One of golf's special appeals is that it can be played two ways. The outcome can be determined on the basis of holes won—match play—or by total number of strokes—stroke play. I prefer stroke play but do not quarrel with the contention that match play is fascinating, calls for a different strategic approach and, above all, is intensely personal.

2-1. Winner of Hole

Rule 2-1 defines match play as the form of the game in which score is kept by the winning of holes rather than by total strokes.

2-2. Halved Hole

Rule 2-2 offers a logical exception to the customary penalty of loss of hole in match play. For example, Player A holes out in 4. His opponent has a putt for a half but A violates a rule before B putts. Let's say A inadvertently moves B's ball, an error which calls for a one-stroke penalty on A. The penalty can't be applied since A already has holed out in 4. Since the best B can do is hole out in 4 himself the hole is automatically halved.

2-3. Winner of Match

In Rule 2-3, think about the phrase "stipulated round." Again, the Definitions can unlock the mysteries of the rules and that's why they are underlined in the text. The "stipulated round" requires that holes be played in numerical sequence, beginning at No. 1. If opponents in a club competition start their match on the 10th hole, they can be disqualified unless the Committee approves.

2-4. Concession of Next Stroke, Hole or Match

As for Rule 2-4, concessions need to be loud and clear. Once a putt is conceded, that's it. The concession cannot be recalled, nor can it be declined. If the player nevertheless putts and misses, it's irrelevant. Exception: If the form of play is four-ball match play, two versus two, a player whose putt has been conceded may not then putt for the purpose of showing his partner the line. If that happens, the partner—the intended beneficiary—is disqualified from that hole.

2-5. Claims

The first sentence of Rule 2-5 deals with the common problem of what to do in a match when opponents differ on a Rule or don't know the answer. They should continue play even though the status of the match is in doubt. The standing of the match will be adjusted according to the answer they receive from the Committee or its agent later.

Focus on the word "claim" in Rule 2-5. It's commonly expressed as "call," i.e., "I call this hole on you." Claims must be timely. If you see your opponent violate a Rule during the second hole, don't bother to bring it up during the third hole. You can't hold your claim in reserve, as Seve Ballesteros learned during the 1991 Ryder Cup Match. Paul Azinger and Chip Beck, playing Seve and Jose Maria Olazabal in foursomes, inadvertently switched brands of balls on the 7th hole in violation of a local rule. Seve didn't mention it until the 10th hole—too late.

On the other hand, if your opponent violated a Rule during the second hole, you didn't know it, but learned of the transgression later, the clock has not run out on your right to make a claim. We'll explore that in Rule 34.

In general, match play violations call for loss of hole. There are some exceptions to that principle. In every case the exceptions are specified in the Rules. A primary example occurs in Rule 18 when a player accidentally moves his ball. It's a one-stroke penalty in match or stroke play, and the ball must be replaced.

Since more than 90 percent of everyday golf is played at match play, it's worth summarizing a variety of match play Decisions:

● Opponents are unsure how to rule, so they agree to treat a hole as halved—even though a violation took place. They are not DQ'd for agreeing to waive a Rule. They were merely ignorant of the Rules and the hole stands as halved.

● Opponents leave the 18th green under the impression that A has won 1 up. Then they realize the match was all square. Since there's no indication wrong information was given, the result stands, with A the winner.

● Two players, in a hurry, agreed to omit the play of two holes in their match, making it into a 16-hole contest. Both are to be DQ'd for failing to play the stipulated round.

● On an unfamiliar course, opponents played three holes out of sequence but discovered the error before the end of the match. The results of the holes played out of sequence are to be disregarded and the match resumed at the proper hole.

● A player concedes an opponent's putt for a 4 and knocks the ball in the hole inadvertently. The opponent claims his score should be 3. No it shouldn't. It's 4.

● A hole is conceded, but then the winner of the hole realizes he played a wrong ball from the rough. What's the deal? In this case, the concession is irrelevant because the player who played a wrong ball lost the hole when he played a wrong ball.

● This one is very subtle: If you see an opponent violate a Rule but don't want to get into a hassle, or want to act in what you feel is a sportsmanlike manner, don't say anything. You may disregard the violation. However, if you say something to the effect that you noticed a violation but are not going to call it, that's trouble. If the opponent accepts your offer, the pair of you have then agreed to waive a Rule.

● A makes a claim. B doesn't dispute it. A wins the match. Two days later B learns that A's claim was erroneous. Too bad! The result stands.

● It's an everyday handicap match and A is getting one stroke from B on the seventh hole. But after the *sixth* hole A says he won the hole because of his lone handicap stroke. B doesn't object. Then, as they play the next hole, they realize A took his stroke on the wrong hole. The result of the sixth hole stands! It was up to B to know where A got his shot. (But if A is a decent person, he may concede the seventh hole to B and walk right to the eighth tee.)

RULE 3

STROKE PLAY

3-1.
Winner

The competitor who plays the stipulated round or rounds in the fewest strokes is the winner.

3-2.
Failure to Hole Out

If a competitor fails to hole out at any hole and does not correct his mistake before he plays a stroke from the next teeing ground or, in the case of the last hole of the round, before he leaves the putting green, *he shall be disqualified.*

a. PROCEDURE

In stroke play only, when during play of a hole a competitor is doubtful of his rights or procedure, he may, without penalty, play a second ball. After the situation which caused the doubt has arisen, the competitor should, before taking further action, announce to his marker or a fellow-competitor his decision to invoke this Rule and the ball with which he will score if the Rules permit.

The competitor shall report the facts to the <u>Committee</u> before returning his score card unless he scores the same with both balls; if he fails to do so, *he shall be disqualified.*

b. DETERMINATION OF SCORE FOR HOLE

If the Rules allow the procedure selected in advance by the competitor, the score with the ball selected shall be his score for the hole.

If the competitor fails to announce in advance his decision to invoke this Rule or his selection, the score with the original ball or, if the original ball is not one of the balls being played, the first ball put into play shall count if the Rules allow the procedure adopted for such ball.

Note: *A second ball played under Rule 3-3 is not a provisional ball under Rule 27-2.*

If a competitor refuses to comply with a Rule affecting the rights of another competitor, *he shall be disqualified.*

The penalty for a breach of a Rule in stroke play is two strokes except when otherwise provided.

3-3.

Doubt as to Procedure

3-4.

Refusal to Comply with a Rule

3-5.

General Penalty

Stroke play is commonly called "medal play"—a term derived from the old British custom of playing one-day competitions for the prize medal. (My permanent prize for winning the 1982 U.S. Open Championship, by the way, is a USGA gold medal.) Golf was originally played only at match play. Stroke play was inspired by the need to finish a tournament in only one day.

3-2. Failure to Hole Out

It is the essence of stroke play that the player return a score for every hole, which means completing the hole.

A classic example occurred on the final green of the 1962 U.S. Open between rookie pro Jack Nicklaus and Arnold Palmer. Palmer graciously picked up Jack's ball marker as an act of concession, but USGA Executive Director Joe Dey insisted that Jack replace the marker and hole out. Otherwise, Jack would not have had a score.

3-3. Doubt as to Procedure

The privilege of playing a second ball exists in stroke play but not in match play. See, the essence of match play is that players know the current status of the match. The introduction of a second ball would erode that principle. The element of strategy in match play goes out the window if a player has to play against two balls, not knowing which one counts.

An application of Rule 3-3 might go like this: Your ball is embedded on the bank of a pond. The grass is closely mown. The Committee has failed to mark the margin of the water hazard, so you can't tell if your ball is in or out of the hazard.

If the ball is within the hazard, you're out of luck. If it's outside the hazard, you are entitled to relief without penalty (see Rule 25-2). So you invoke Rule 3-3 by telling your marker you intend to play both the original and a second ball. And don't forget to state which ball you want to count. If you fail to say, the score made with the original ball will count.

Then play both balls into the hole, the first under the premise that the ball was plugged inside the hazard (no relief) and the second as if you were entitled to a free drop.

When you've finished the round, dump the case into the lap of the Committee. It's up to them to decide whether your original ball was within the hazard.

3-4. Refusal to Comply with a Rule

I've never seen an occasion when this Rule had to be invoked. But it might be there for a reason. An extreme case might be that of a player refusing to lift this ball when asked to do so by a fellow-competitor whose line was interfered with by the ball.

3-5. General Penalty

The general penalty in stroke play is two strokes, just as in match play it's loss of hole. But some transgressions call for disqualification. One example is practicing on the course on the day of a competition. There is one important one-stroke penalty: when a player, his partner or a caddie accidentally moves the player's ball.

CLUBS AND THE BALL

The United States Golf Association and the Royal and Ancient Golf Club of St. Andrews reserve the right to change the Rules and make and change the interpretations relating to clubs, balls and other implements at any time.

RULE 4

CLUBS

If there may be any reasonable basis for doubt as to whether a club which is to be manufactured conforms with Rule 4 and Appendix II*, the manufacturer should submit a sample to the United States Golf Association for a ruling, such sample to become its property for reference purposes. If a manufacturer fails to do so, he assumes the risk of a ruling that the club does not conform with the Rules of Golf.

A player in doubt as to the conformity of a club should consult the United States Golf Association.

A club is an implement designed to be used for striking the ball.

A putter is a club designed primarily for use on the putting green.

The player's clubs shall conform with the provisions of this Rule and with the specifications and interpretations set forth in Appendix II.

a. GENERAL

The club shall be composed of a shaft and a head. All parts of

4-1.
Form and Make of Clubs

---

*Hereafter when in the text of the Rules themselves reference is made to Appendix II & III, please note that these may be found in the USGA's *Rules of Golf* booklet.

the club shall be fixed so that the club is one unit. The club shall not be designed to be adjustable except for weight. The club shall not be substantially different from the traditional and customary form and make.

b. SHAFT

The shaft shall be generally straight, with the same bending and twisting properties in any direction, and shall be attached to the clubhead at the heel either directly or through a single plain neck or socket. A putter shaft may be attached to any point in the head.

c. GRIP

The grip consists of that part of the shaft designed to be held by the player and any material added to it for the purpose of obtaining a firm hold. The grip shall be substantially straight and plain in form and shall not be molded for any part of the hands.

d. CLUBHEAD

The distance from the heel to the toe of the clubhead shall be greater than the distance from the face to the back. The clubhead shall be generally plain in shape.

The clubhead shall have only one face designed for striking the ball, except that a putter may have two such faces if their characteristics are the same, they are opposite each other and the loft of each is the same and does not exceed 10 degrees.

e. CLUB FACE

The face shall not have any degree of concavity and, in relation to the ball, shall be hard and rigid. It shall be generally smooth except for such markings as are permitted by Appendix II.

f. WEAR

A club which conforms with Rule 4-1 when new is deemed to conform after wear through normal use. Any part of a club which has been purposely altered is regarded as new and must conform, in the altered state, with the Rules.

g. DAMAGE

If a player's club ceases to conform with Rule 4-1 because of damage sustained in the normal course of play, the player may:

(i) use the club in its damaged state, but only for the remainder of the <u>stipulated round</u> during which such damage was sustained; or

(ii) without unduly delaying play, repair it.

A club which ceases to conform because of damage sustained other than in the normal course of play shall not subsequently be used during the round.

(Damage changing playing characteristics of club — see Rule 4-2.)

(Damage rendering club unfit for play — see Rule 4-4a.)

4-2.
Playing Characteristics Changed

During a <u>stipulated round</u>, the playing characteristics of a club shall not be purposely changed by adjustment or by any other means.

If the playing characteristics of a player's club are changed during a round because of damage sustained in the normal course of play, the player may:

Rulings on Clubs

These five clubs were submitted to the USGA for rulings. Only the club in the center conforms. From left to right, here's why the other four do not: (1) the arrow feature means that the neck is not "plain"; (2) it's got more than one neck or socket; (4) it's got a centered shaft, a feature OK only on putters; (5) that's a concave face. (R. 4)

(i) use the club in its altered state; or

(ii) without unduly delaying play, repair it.

If the playing characteristics of a player's club are changed because of damage sustained other than in the normal course of play, the club shall not subsequently be used during the round.

Damage to a club which occurred prior to a round may be repaired during the round, provided the playing characteristics are not changed and play is not unduly delayed.

No foreign material shall be applied to the club face for the purpose of influencing the movement of the ball.

PENALTY FOR BREACH OF RULE 4-1, -2 or -3:

Disqualification.

4-3.

Foreign Material

33

4-4.

Maximum of Fourteen Clubs

a. SELECTION AND REPLACEMENT OF CLUBS

The player shall start a <u>stipulated round</u> with not more than fourteen clubs. He is limited to the clubs thus selected for that round except that, without unduly delaying play, he may:

(i) if he started with fewer than fourteen, add as many as will bring his total to that number; and

(ii) replace, with any club, a club which becomes unfit for play in the normal course of play.

The addition or replacement of a club or clubs may not be made by borrowing any club selected for play by any other person playing on the course.

b. PARTNERS MAY SHARE CLUBS

Partners may share clubs, provided that the total number of clubs carried by the partners so sharing does not exceed fourteen.

PENALTY FOR BREACH OF RULE 4-4a or b,
REGARDLESS OF NUMBER OF EXCESS CLUBS CARRIED:

Match play — At the conclusion of the hole at which the breach is discovered, the state of the match shall be adjusted by deducting one hole for each hole at which a breach occurred. Maximum deduction per round: two holes.

Stroke play — Two strokes for each hole at which any breach occurred; maximum penalty per round: four strokes.

Bogey and par competitions — Penalties as in match play.

Stableford competitions — See Note to Rule 32-1b.

c. EXCESS CLUB DECLARED OUT OF PLAY

Any club carried or used in breach of this Rule shall be declared out of play by the player immediately upon discovery that a breach has occurred and thereafter shall not be used by the player during the round.

PENALTY FOR BREACH OF RULE 4-4c: *Disqualification.*

Rules 4 and 5 are often referred to as "the equipment rules" as distinct from all the others—the "playing rules." Golf is a game in which a ball is played into a hole with clubs. Inevitably, there have to be definitions of what a ball and a club are. That's what Rules 4 and 5 do.

The purpose in establishing standards is to preserve both the challenge and the tradition of the game. There are those who say the USGA and R&A have allowed technology to take over the game. Others say the equipment rules are too severe.

It's an endless argument, one that has bred a dreadful amount of litigation in recent years. One thing is certain: The USGA and R&A, as nonprofit entities, have no financial axes to grind and approach the subject of what equipment should be without bias.

4-1. Form and Make of Clubs

There are golfers who worry that their grooves become too wide through wear. Not to worry. Rule 4-1 affirms that the club conforms so long as it conformed when new and that it was altered from normal use.

4-2. Playing Characteristics Changed

An example of a violation would be the addition of lead tape to a driver *during* a round so as to change its weight and feel.

4-3. Foreign Material

This prohibition stops imaginative golfers from applying materials such as chalk or oily substances on club faces in the hope that the ball will go longer or straighter from reduced spin—a dubious notion. But I still recall fondly a teammate of mine on the Stanford University golf team, one Sandy Adelman, who spit with great relish on the face of his driver before every tee shot. Sandy might not agree, but a Decision says that "saliva is considered a foreign material."

4-4. Maximum of Fourteen Clubs

There was no limit on the number of clubs until 1938. A maximum was established because some players had gone to extremes in terms of carrying "specialty" clubs, supposedly designed to fit every kind of shot. Golf bags became arsenals. Lawson Little and Craig Wood, stars of the 1930s, both went forth to battle with 25 clubs.

Iron Bryon

There's no other machine exactly like the USGA's Iron Byron, the USGA's mechanical golfer, which plays on a course all its own—a test range at USGA headquarters. The prototype was built to emulate the swing of my friend and mentor Byron Nelson. The USGA machine is rigged with a laser beam and high-speed photo equipment. Every hit is dissected to the extent of a recording of the speed of the club at impact (in millionths of a second) and wind velocity (both horizontally and vertically) during the six seconds the ball is in flight.

During the USGA Overall Distance Standard tests, a ball is teed just after being removed from an incubator where it was stored at 75°F. When the clubhead strikes the ball, it will be moving at 109 miles per hour—about the clubhead speed of a long driver on the Tour. (R. 4-1)

The number fourteen was selected because it corresponded with what was generally considered a standard set. It used to be common on the PGA Tour for most players to carry irons numbered 1 through 9, a putter, two wedges and two woods. But now you often see bags with three wedges—the third is one with extra loft. That means one of the other irons has to go.

Applying penalties for violations of Rule 4-4 is tricky. Suppose, in a match, player A is 2 up against B after 16 holes. They learn on the 17th tee that A has been carrying a 15th club. The status of the match immediately goes to all square since A suffers the maximum penalty—loss of two holes.

Another example: A wins the first hole of her match against B, who then learns she's toting an extra club. Poor B goes from 1 down to 2 down even though she's only played one hole. Incidentally, they don't skip the second hole; the match resumes on the second tee with the penalty added.

There's a change in Rule 4-4 effective in 1992. If a player is entitled to replace or add a club (having broken one in the normal course of play or having started out with fewer than fourteen), that addition cannot be made by borrowing a club selected for play from anyone else playing the course. The replacement is likely to come from the golf shop.

Just about every player I know has carried an extra club or more at some time. It happened to me once—in a qualifying round for the Missouri Amateur Championship. I managed somehow to go out with eighteen clubs. At that time the penalty was more severe than now. It called for a maximum of four penalty strokes for every extra club. So my nifty 76 was converted into a 92. That's the last time I or my caddie failed to count clubs on the first tee.

RULE 5

THE BALL

5-1.
General

The ball the player uses shall conform to specifications set forth in Appendix III on maximum weight, minimum size, spherical symmetry, initial velocity and overall distance when tested under specified conditions.

5-2.
Foreign Material

No foreign material shall be applied to a ball for the purpose of changing its playing characteristics.
PENALTY FOR BREACH OF RULE 5-1 OR 5-2: *Disqualification.*

5-3.
Ball Unfit for Play

A ball is unfit for play if it is visibly cut, cracked or out of shape. A ball is not unfit for play solely because mud or other materials adhere to it, its surface is scratched or scraped or its paint is damaged or discolored.

If a player has reason to believe his ball has become unfit for play during the play of the hole being played, he may during the play of such hole lift his ball without penalty to determine whether it is unfit.

Before lifting the ball, the player must announce his intention to his opponent in match play or his marker or a fellow-competitor in stroke play and mark the position of the ball. He may then lift and examine the ball without cleaning it and must give his opponent, marker or fellow-competitor an opportunity to examine the ball.

If he fails to comply with this procedure, *he shall incur a penalty of one stroke.*

If it is determined that the ball has become unfit for play during play of the hole being played, the player may substitute another ball, placing it on the spot where the original ball lay. Otherwise, the original ball shall be replaced.

If a ball breaks into pieces as a result of a stroke, the stroke shall be cancelled and the player shall play a ball without penalty as nearly as possible at the spot from which the original ball was played (see Rule 20-5).

*Penalty for Breach of Rule 5-3:

Match play — Loss of hole; Stroke play — Two strokes.

If a player incurs the general penalty for breach of Rule 5-3, no additional penalty under the Rule shall be applied.

Note: *If the opponent, marker or fellow-competitor wishes to dispute a claim of unfitness, he must do so before the player plays another ball.*

(Cleaning ball lifted from putting green or under any other Rule — see Rule 21.)

There are more than 700 types of golf balls that conform to the Rules of Golf. When a ball fails to conform, it's invariably a case of a manufacturing error that shifts the product ever so slightly over the wrong side of the line of one of the standards.

The five standards are:

• Maximum weight of 1.68 ounces. The ball would go farther if it was a little heavier.

• Minimum size of 1.68 inches in diameter. Again, there would be a distance advantage for a slightly smaller ball, especially into the wind.

• Spherical symmetry, as measured in a sophisticated outdoor test. It exists to prevent the possibility of a "self-correcting" pattern of flight.

• Initial velocity, measured on an indoor device, imposes a limit on a ball's initial resiliency and thus to its distance.

• Overall distance, performed outdoors using the USGA robot "Iron Byron," named for my friend Byron Nelson.

The test restricts the distance a ball can be hit with a driver. That doesn't mean long-hitter John Daly, winner of the 1991 PGA Championship, can't outhit the machine, which is set up to carry balls about 255 yards to a range that affords another 25 to 30 yards of roll. What the test does assure is stability. If the force of a given swing is enough to achieve a distance of 285 yards today, you can be sure that the same swing is not going to be allowed to propel a ball 305 yards 10 or 20 years from now.

I'm finicky about the balls I use. Most Tour players put a new ball into play every fourth hole. Moreover, I am inclined to replace a ball after scarring its cover with a bunker shot, so I average eight balls a round. Of course, neither I nor my Tour brethren have to pay for balls.

You may have heard of the "one-ball rule." Actually, that's a permissible "condition of play" used on the highest competitive level of the game—in national championships and certainly on the PGA Tour. It restricts a player to one type of ball during a round. The "one-ball rule" is almost never used, nor should it be used, in everyday play or in club tournaments.

PLAYER'S RESPONSIBILITIES

THE PLAYER

Definition

A "marker" is one who is appointed by the Committee to record a <u>competitor's</u> score in stroke play. He may be a <u>fellow-competitor</u>. He is not a <u>referee</u>.

6·1.
Conditions of Competition

The player is responsible for knowing the conditions under which the competition is to be played (Rule 33-1).

6·2.
Handicap

a. MATCH PLAY
Before starting a match in a handicap competition, the players should determine from one another their respective handicaps. If a player begins the match having declared a higher handicap which would affect the number of strokes given or received, *he shall be disqualified;* otherwise, the player shall play off the declared handicap.

b. STROKE PLAY
In any round of a handicap competition, the competitor shall ensure that his handicap is recorded on his score card before it is returned to the Committee. If no handicap is recorded on his score card before it is returned, or if the recorded handicap is higher than that to which he is entitled and this affects the number of strokes received, *he shall be disqualified* from that round of the handicap competition; otherwise, the score shall stand.

Note: *It is the player's responsibility to know the holes at which handicap strokes are to be given or received.*

6·3.
Time of Starting and Groups

a. TIME OF STARTING
The player shall start at the time laid down by the Committee.

b. GROUPS

In stroke play, the competitor shall remain throughout the round in the group arranged by the Committee unless the Committee authorizes or ratifies a change.

PENALTY FOR BREACH OF RULE 6-3: *Disqualification.*

(Best-ball and four-ball play — see Rules 30-3a and 31-2.)

Note: *The Committee may provide in the conditions of a competition (Rule 33-1) that, if the player arrives at his starting point, ready to play, within five minutes after his starting time, in the absence of circumstances which warrant waiving the penalty of disqualification as provided in Rule 33-7, the penalty for failure to start on time is* loss of the first hole in match play or two strokes at the first hole in stroke play *instead of disqualification.*

The player may have only one <u>caddie</u> at any one time, *under penalty of disqualification.*

For any breach of a Rule by his caddie, the player incurs the applicable penalty.

6-4.
Caddie

The responsibility for playing the proper ball rests with the player. Each player should put an identification mark on his ball.

6-5.
Ball

a. RECORDING SCORES

After each hole the <u>marker</u> should check the score with the competitor and record it. On completion of the round the marker shall sign the card and hand it to the competitor. If more than one marker records the scores, each shall sign for the part for which he is responsible.

b. SIGNING AND RETURNING CARD

After completion of the round, the competitor should check his score for each hole and settle any doubtful points with the Committee. He shall ensure that the marker has signed the card, countersign the card himself and return it to the Committee as soon as possible.

PENALTY FOR BREACH OF RULE 6-6b: *Disqualification.*

c. ALTERATION OF CARD

No alteration may be made on a card after the competitor has returned it to the Committee.

d. WRONG SCORE FOR HOLE

The competitor is responsible for the correctness of the score recorded for each hole. If he returns a score for any hole lower than actually taken, *he shall be disqualified.* If he returns a score for any hole higher than actually taken, the score as returned shall stand.

Note 1: *The Committee is responsible for the addition of scores and application of the handicap recorded on the card — see Rule 33-5.*

Note 2: *In four-ball stroke play, see also Rule 31-4 and -7a.*

6-6.
Scoring in Stroke Play

The player shall play without undue delay. Between completion of a hole and playing from the next teeing ground, the player shall not unduly delay play.

6-7.
Undue Delay

39

PENALTY FOR BREACH OF RULE 6-7:
Match play — Loss of hole; Stroke play — Two strokes.
For repeated offense — Disqualification.
If the player unduly delays play between holes, he is delaying the play of the next hole and the penalty applies to that hole.

6-8.
Discontinuance of Play

a. WHEN PERMITTED
The player shall not discontinue play unless:
(i) the Committee has suspended play;
(ii) he believes there is danger from lightning;
(iii) he is seeking a decision from the Committee on a doubtful or disputed point (see Rules 2-5 and 34-3); or
(iv) there is some other good reason such as sudden illness.
Bad weather is not of itself a good reason for discontinuing play.
If the player discontinues play without specific permission from the Committee, he shall report to the Committee as soon as practicable. If he does so and the Committee considers his reason satisfactory, the player incurs no penalty. Otherwise, *the player shall be disqualified.*
Exception in match play: Players discontinuing match play by agreement are not subject to disqualification unless by so doing the competition is delayed.
Note: *Leaving the course does not of itself constitute discontinuance of play.*
b. PROCEDURE WHEN PLAY SUSPENDED BY COMMITTEE
When play is suspended by the Committee, if the players in a match or group are between the play of two holes, they shall not resume play until the Committee has ordered a resumption of play. If they are in the process of playing a hole, they may continue provided they do so without delay. If they choose to continue, they shall discontinue either before or immediately after completing the hole, and shall not thereafter resume play until the Committee has ordered a resumption of play.
When play has been suspended by the Committee, the player shall resume play when the Committee has ordered a resumption of play.
PENALTY FOR BREACH OF RULE 6-8b: *Disqualification.*
c. LIFTING BALL WHEN PLAY DISCONTINUED
When during the play of a hole a player discontinues play under Rule 6-8a, he may lift his ball. A ball may be cleaned when so lifted. If a ball has been so lifted, the player shall, when play is resumed, place a ball on the spot from which the original ball was lifted.
PENALTY FOR BREACH OF RULE 6-8c:
Match play — Loss of hole; Stroke play — Two strokes.

Rule 6 contains a mix of items underscoring the tenet that golf, unlike team sports, requires the players to do more than go out and play. The player is responsible for knowing the conditions, or terms, of the event and the Rules themselves.

6-1. Conditions of Competition
Golf administrators use the phrase "conditions of play." They include

the essentials: the form of play (match or stroke, individual or team); whether or not it's a handicap event and, if so, in what form; who is eligible; the dates and starting times; whether there's an entry fee; and the prizes. It's the job of the Committee to establish and announce the conditions; it's up to the player to know them.

6-2. Handicap

The USGA Handicap System now expresses handicaps in one decimal; e.g., 10.8. That's the golfer's Handicap Index—the basic number. That Index must be converted into strokes received by using a chart posted in the locker room or golf shop of virtually every course. It's called the Slope chart.

The number of strokes received varies. The 10.8 golfer might receive 11, 12 or even more strokes on a course with a high Slope rating; but only 10 or less strokes if the course has a low Slope rating.

The golfer doesn't have to know the first thing about the way in which the USGA Handicap System, including Slope, is constructed. But, for the curious, it's all laid out in a booklet called the "USGA Handicap System and Golf Committee Manual." The USGA will send you one for $7.25.

6-3. Time of Starting and Groups

Every so often, even on great occasions, a player will miss his starting time. The penalty is disqualification. It happened to Seve Ballesteros in the 1980 U.S. Open Championship.

A Committee may waive the disqualification penalty for good cause. Examples? You stop on way to the course to rescue a child from a burning building. But running out of gas, or "The wake-up call system didn't work" are examples of personal failures that should not cut it with a Committee.

6-4. Caddie

A player and his caddie are an intimate unit; they share responsibility for upholding the Rules. If a caddie accidentally steps on a scuff mark on his player's line of putt, the player is penalized.

Here are some examples of acts a caddie may perform: Search for a ball; place the player's clubs in a hazard; repair ball marks and old hole plugs; remove loose impediments on the line of putt or elsewhere; mark the position of a ball; clean the player's ball; remove movable obstructions.

6-5. Ball

The words "should" and "shall" are sprinkled throughout the Rules. In this case, "should" tells you it's no violation if you don't put a distinctive mark on your ball, but you're silly not to. Suppose you are playing Brand X with a number 1 on it. You yank your drive into the rough where, lo and behold, there are two Brand X 1 balls. What you've got now is a lost ball unless you can with certainty say which is yours. My personal marking code consists of a couple of pencil marks in the dimple to the right of the number. An indelible pen also does the job nicely.

6-6. Scoring in Stroke Play

There's a section devoted only to stroke play scoring because match play depends entirely on the opponents' agreement as to the status of the match. It might be wise or useful to keep a card in match play, but it has no official status and does not have to be turned in. The Committee only needs to know who won.

In stroke play, there must be a "marker" identified by the Committee. The marker invariably is another player in the same group. This is so, both in club events and on the Tour where a volunteer scorer also goes around with the players. The scorer's role is as the source of information for scoreboards and the media. Ultimately, what's on the card kept by the marker is what counts. When I finish a round, I always double-check the card kept by my marker with the unofficial scorer after going over it myself.

Every season someone forgets to sign a scorecard in a million dollar tournament and is disqualified, a penalty that underscores the importance of individual responsibility in golf. So far I've not been disqualified for either turning in an incorrect card or failing to sign one.

The most famous and sad application of Rule 6-6 happened in the 1968 Masters Tournament. Robert De Vicenzo of Argentina should have tied Bob Goalby for first place, but Roberto, who made a birdie 3 on the 17th hole, countersigned the card handed to him by his marker Tommy Aaron without reviewing it carefully. Aaron inadvertently put down a "4" for Roberto on the 17th. When the card was signed and returned to the Committee, the higher score had to stand.

I'm very happy with the strictness of Rule 6-6, thank you. It gives me the absolute responsibility for my score. I don't have to sign for the card until and unless I'm satisfied that the numbers show what I shot. Any alteration of the Rule would erode that right.

6-7. Undue Delay

I'm proud of my reputation as one of the game's relatively fast players. Golf has been allowed to become much too slow. Defining "undue delay" has always been a problem. The USGA and the Tour now use similar timing systems, but I think these systems are too lenient since they allow players 45 seconds, and sometimes more, to make a stroke after the coast is clear. That's too long.

6-8. Discontinuance of Play

When to discontinue play? Hard rain alone is not sufficient cause so long as the course remains playable. But note the general exception to the effect that in match play opponents can by mutual agreement suspend play, providing they don't cause the competition to be delayed.

Lightning, of course, is another story. Play should be stopped at the first *hint* of lightning. Rule 6-8 gives the player the right to stop "when he believes there is danger from lightning." He doesn't have to consult with or get the approval of his opponents, fellow-competitors or the Committee.

If any of us needed to be reminded of the perils of lightning, we were given the terrible examples of the deaths of spectators struck by lightning during the 1991 U.S. Open and PGA Championships.

The USGA publishes a poster on protection during lightning on a golf course. It should be displayed in every locker room.

RULE 7

PRACTICE

a. MATCH PLAY

On any day of a match play competition, a player may practice on the competition course before a round.

b. STROKE PLAY

On any day of a stroke competition or play-off, a competitor shall not practice on the competition course or test the surface of any putting green on the course before a round or play-off. When two or more rounds of a stroke competition are to be played over consecutive days, practice between those rounds on any competition course remaining to be played is prohibited.

Exception: Practice putting or chipping on or near the first teeing ground before starting a round or play-off is permitted.

PENALTY FOR BREACH OF RULE 7-1b: *Disqualification.*

Note: *The Committee may in the conditions of a competition (Rule 33-1) prohibit practice on the competition course on any day of a match play competition or permit practice on the competition course or part of the course (Rule 33-2c) on any day of or between rounds of a stroke competition.*

A player shall not play a practice stroke either during the play of a hole or between the play of two holes except that, between the play of two holes, the player may practice putting or chipping on or near the putting green of the hole last played, any practice putting green or the teeing ground of the next hole to be played in the round, provided such practice stroke is not played from a hazard and does not unduly delay play (Rule 6-7).

Exception: When play has been suspended by the Committee, a player may, prior to resumption of play, practice (a) as provided in this Rule, (b) anywhere other than on the competition course and (c) as otherwise permitted by the Committee.

PENALTY FOR BREACH OF RULE 7-2:

Match play — Loss of hole; Stroke play — Two strokes.

In the event of a breach between the play of two holes, the penalty applies to the next hole.

Note 1: *A practice swing is not a practice stroke and may be taken at any place, provided the player does not breach the Rules.*

Note 2: *The Committee may prohibit practice on or near the putting green of the hole last played.*

7-1.
Before or Between Rounds

7-2.
During Round

7-1. Before or During Rounds

The restrictions against practicing on the course are markedly different in the two basic forms of play.

In match play, you are not prohibited from practicing on the course prior to a round, presumably because opponents obviously start at the same time and therefore have the same opportunity to explore the course. But in stroke play, those with early starting times would be disadvantaged.

Watch out for Rule 7-1 if you're ever involved in a 36-hole stroke play qualifier. You may play the first round Saturday morning and decide to practice some on the course in the afternoon prior to Sunday's second round. Don't! The penalty is disqualification unless the committee specifically stipulated otherwise.

7-2. During Round

Rule 7-2 allows for such innocuous acts as chipping near or on a tee when you're delayed. It also permits you to practice-putt on the hole you've just completed—providing you don't delay play unduly. But you can never play a practice stroke from any hazard.

Note 2 at the end of this Rule is used on the Tour, i.e., practice putting is prohibited because it might delay play and the added traffic would roughen the greens around the hole.

The application of Rule 7-2 is curious. Penalties apply to the next hole. Suppose a player replays a bunker shot after the fourth hole is over, and he's just halved that hole. The player loses the fifth hole, not the fourth, which means he and his opponent skip the fifth hole and go directly to the sixth tee.

Here are the summaries of two key Decisions illustrating what Rule 7-2 is all about:

• A player drops a ball in a fairway and putts it. Violation!

• A player backhands some balls from the fairway, back toward the adjacent driving range. No violation, not for the casual flicking of a ball in order to tidy up; but if the player's intent is to smooth out his swing, that's practicing.

RULE 8

ADVICE; INDICATING LINE OF PLAY

Definitions

"Advice" is any counsel or suggestion which could influence a player in determining his play, the choice of a club or the method of making a stroke.

Information on the Rules or on matters of public information, such as the position of hazards or the flagstick on the putting green, is not advice.

The "line of play" is the direction which the player wishes his ball to take after a stroke, plus a reasonable distance on either side of the intended direction. The line of play extends vertically upwards from the ground, but does not extend beyond the hole.

8-1.

Advice

A player shall not give advice to anyone in the competition except his partner. A player may ask for advice from only his partner or either of their caddies.

8-2.

a. OTHER THAN ON PUTTING GREEN

Except on the putting green, a player may have the line of

play indicated to him by anyone, but no one shall stand on or close to the line while the stroke is being played. Any mark placed during the play of a hole by the player or with his knowledge to indicate the line shall be removed before the stroke is played.

Exception: Flagstick attended or held up — see Rule 17-1.

b. ON THE PUTTING GREEN

When the player's ball is on the putting green, the player, his partner or either of their caddies may, before but not during the stroke, point out a line for putting, but in so doing the putting green shall not be touched. No mark shall be placed anywhere to indicate a line for putting.

PENALTY FOR BREACH OF RULE:

Match play — Loss of hole; Stroke play — Two strokes.

Note: *In a team competition with or without concurrent individual competition, the Committee may in the conditions of the competition (Rule 33-1) permit each team to appoint one person, e.g., team captain or coach, who may give advice (including pointing out a line for putting) to members of that team. Such person shall be identified to the Committee prior to the start of the competition.*

8-l. Advice

The vogue for knowing yardages leads to some fine distinctions as to what constitutes "advice." Two key Decisions say:

• It's OK to ask *anyone* the distance from a *permanent object* to the center of the green. That is to say, you can ask what the distance is from a tree, bunker or a sprinkler head to a point on the green.

• It's a violation if you ask someone other than your caddie or partner the distance from a *ball* to the green.

Some other landmark interpretations of Rule 8:

• It's not a violation to look into another player's bag to see what club he used, but if a player wants to keep his club selection a secret by cloaking his clubs with a towel you can't go the extreme of removing the towel.

• If a player tells his opponent or a fellow-competitor during a round that he is overswinging, that constitutes advice however friendly the intent. The beneficiary is not penalized. You can't be faulted for what you hear.

• When a caddie carries clubs for two players, one player may ask the caddie what club the caddies' other employer just used—even though the other player is not a partner.

I have had some problems with the advice Rule. In a National Amateur Championship I yelled across a fairway to ask another young amateur what club he had just played. I was totally ignorant of the Rule, was overheard by a shocked USGA official and properly penalized two strokes.

A dozen years later, I was in the process of winning the Tournament of Champions. I was paired with Lee Trevino who was struggling. I thought I noticed a little swing flaw and told Lee about it. That comment was overheard by Bob Goalby, who was walking the fairway as a TV reporter. Goalby reported what had happened as an illustration of the kind of generosity of spirit that prevails on the Tour. TV viewers recognized what had happened as a violation of the advice Rule. I was penalized two strokes. Thank goodness I had a three-stroke lead.

Brave the Elements
*The Rules do not permit what's
happening here. A player
cannot be shielded from the
elements in the act of making a
stroke. (R. 14-2)*

That incident, which took place in 1980, I believe to have been the first of the so-called "instant replay" rulings generated by television viewers.

8-2. Indicating Line of Play

Rule 8-2 is simple enough. When you can't see what you're aiming at, anyone can help you by indicating the line to the target. But before you play the stroke, your helper has to get off that line. *But* the flagstick itself can be held aloft as you play a stroke, provided it's held above the hole to indicate the position of the hole and not some line to the side of the hole.

On the putting green, the line of play is sacred ground. Rule 8-2b is infringed when caddies or partners touch the green with a club or flagstick pointing out what they consider to be the line. And note that the line is not simply a straight line from the ball to the hole. It's the direction which the player wishes his ball to take, plus a "reasonable" distance on either side of the intended direction.

During John Daly's storybook victory in the 1991 PGA Championship, he nearly ran afoul of this prohibition. His caddie touched the green with the flagstick as Daly was lining up his putt, but PGA officials properly ruled no violation since it was not the caddie's purpose to indicate the line of play. The caddie was just being a touch careless.

RULE 9

INFORMATION AS TO STROKES TAKEN

The number of strokes a player has taken shall include any penalty strokes incurred.

9-1.
General

A player who has incurred a penalty shall inform his opponent as soon as practicable, unless he is obviously proceeding under a Rule involving a penalty and this has been observed by his opponent. If he fails so to inform his opponent, he shall be deemed to have given wrong information, even if he was not aware that he had incurred a penalty.

9-2.
Match Play

An opponent is entitled to ascertain from the player, during the play of a hole, the number of strokes he has taken and, after play of a hole, the number of strokes taken on the hole just completed.

If during the play of a hole the player gives or is deemed to give wrong information as to the number of strokes taken, he shall incur no penalty if he corrects the mistake before his opponent has played his next stroke. If the player fails so to correct the wrong information, *he shall lose the hole.*

If after play of a hole the player gives or is deemed to give wrong information as to the number of strokes taken on the hole just completed and this affects the opponent's understanding of the result of the hole, he shall incur no penalty if he corrects his mistake before any player plays from the next teeing ground or, in the case of the last hole of the match, before all players leave the putting green. If the player fails so to correct the wrong information, *he shall lose the hole.*

A competitor who has incurred a penalty should inform his marker as soon as practicable.

9-3.
Stroke Play

The language of Rule 9-2 was clarified for the 1992 version of the Rules of Golf.

During a match it's essential that both parties be immediately aware of penalties. It's long been a violation for a player who has suffered a penalty not to inform his opponent. The Rule now makes it clear, however, that the suffering player doesn't have to state the obvious. If a player knocks his

ball into a water hazard in full view of his opponent, there's no need for words. On the other hand, if the penalty comes from an action out of view of the opponent, the opponent must be advised "as soon as practicable."

The word "deemed" is a favorite in the Rules. It means, in the context of Rule 9, that a failure to announce you've incurred a penalty is the same as being asked how many strokes you've taken, and coming up with the wrong answer. That's called giving "wrong information."

Here's an example of how wrong information applies after the fact: A player thinks he won the fifth hole but realizes during the play of the sixth hole that he played a wrong ball on the fifth. The status of the match should be adjusted belatedly; i.e., the player lost the fifth hole for playing a wrong ball.

And ignorance of the Rules is never an excuse. Example: your opponent removes a stone in a bunker on the ninth hole, but you don't see that. The hole is seemingly won by him. As you stroll down the 10th fairway, he casually remarks that he was able to make a good bunker shot back on 9

Indicating Line of Play
My caddie, or for that matter anyone else, can show me the line (left) to the hole, but he isn't allowed to stand on or near the line while the stroke is being played. He's moved off the line in the picture at right. (R. 8-2)

because he removed a stone. You may claim the ninth hole on the grounds that your opponent removed a loose impediment in a hazard.

By not revealing the violation (even though he didn't know there was a violation) he gave you wrong information. He lost the hole. Instead of being 1 down, you are now 1 up.

ORDER OF PLAY

ORDER OF PLAY

10-1.
Match Play

a. TEEING GROUND

The side entitled to play first from the <u>teeing ground</u> is said to have the "honor."

The side which shall have the honor at the first teeing ground shall be determined by the order of the draw. In the absence of a draw, the honor should be decided by lot.

The side which wins a hole shall take the honor at the next teeing ground. If a hole has been halved, the side which had the honor at the previous teeing ground shall retain it.

b. OTHER THAN ON TEEING GROUND

When the balls are in play, the ball farther from the hole shall be played first. If the balls are equidistant from the hole, the ball to be played first should be decided by lot.

Exception: Rule 30-3c (best-ball and four-ball match play).

c. PLAYING OUT OF TURN

If a player plays when his opponent should have played, the opponent may immediately require the player to cancel the stroke so played and, in correct order, play a ball without penalty as nearly as possible at the spot from which the original ball was last played (see Rule 20-5).

10-2.
Stroke Play

a. TEEING GROUND

The competitor entitled to play first from the <u>teeing ground</u> is said to have the "honor."

The competitor who shall have the honor at the first teeing ground shall be determined by the order of the draw. In the absence of a draw, the honor should be decided by lot.

The competitor with the lowest score at a hole shall take the honor at the next teeing ground. The competitor with the second lowest score shall play next and so on. If two or more competitors have the same score at a hole, they shall play from the next teeing ground in the same order as at the previous teeing ground.

b. OTHER THAN ON TEEING GROUND

When the balls are in play, the ball farthest from the hole shall be played first. If two or more balls are equidistant from the hole, the ball to be played first should be decided by lot.

Exceptions: Rules 22 (ball interfering with or assisting play) and 31-5 (four-ball stroke play).

c. PLAYING OUT OF TURN

If a competitor plays out of turn, no penalty is incurred and the ball shall be played as it lies. If, however, the Committee determines that competitors have agreed to play in an order other than

Nudged Off the Tee

There's no penalty when a ball falls or is knocked off a tee before *a stroke. The ball* may be *teed again. Remember, there can be no stroke without intent.* (R. 11-3)

that set forth in Clauses 2a and 2b of this Rule to give one of them an advantage, *they shall be disqualified.*

(Incorrect order of play in threesomes and foursomes stroke play — see Rule 29-3.)

10-3.
Provisional Ball or Second Ball from Teeing Ground

If a player plays a <u>provisional ball</u> or a second ball from a <u>teeing ground</u>, he should do so after his opponent or fellow-competitor has played his first <u>stroke</u>. If a player plays a provisional ball or a second ball out of turn, Clauses 1c and 2c of this Rule shall apply.

10-4.
Ball Moved in Measuring

If a ball is moved in measuring to determine which ball is farther from the hole, no penalty is incurred and the ball shall be replaced.

Rule 10 expresses the principle that the ball farther from the hole shall be played first. Following is a summary of the consequences when a ball is played out of turn:

● Match play: No penalty, but the opponent may immediately require the player who played out of turn to replay the stroke.

● Stroke play: No penalty, and the ball is played as it then lies—not played over. *But* if there's a conspiracy in order to give one player an advantage, all bets are off. Example: It's a par-3 hole over water with the wind howling. The player who has the honor is uncertain. His friend says, "I'll hit first so you can get a better idea." If he does without objection, both players are disqualified.

Most everyday golf is a form of match play with handicaps. The honor is determined by the net scores of the preceding holes. But in stroke play played at handicap, the gross score of each hole—not the net score— determines the honor. That's because the handicap allowances in stroke play are considered at the end of the round in total. There is no net score for one hole.

Here are a few enlightening Decisions on the subject:

● Two players are in the same ground-under-repair area. The player who was away in the ground under repair is closer to the hole after both players take relief. Who plays next? The player who was away originally; i.e., before relief was taken.

● This time two players have to take relief from the same water hazard. The order of play is determined by where the balls lie; again, not by where they last crossed the margin of the hazard, nor where they drop after taking relief. If they can't figure out which ball in the hazard is "away," they should flip a coin to decide the order of play.

● Here's one, which applies in stroke play, that I just learned, and it's one that is common on the Tour. Let's say I've just run a 40-foot putt three feet past the hole. I prefer to putt, an act generally condoned in stroke play since it speeds up play but my fellow-competitor objects. I can do so, but *not* if I lift my ball and clean it. If I lift the ball and then putt, I have technically violated Rule 10-2b; however, there is no penalty.

TEEING GROUND

TEEING GROUND

The "teeing ground" is the starting place for the hole to be played. It is a rectangular area two club-lengths in depth, the front and the sides of which are defined by the outside limits of two tee-markers. A ball is outside the teeing ground when all of it lies outside the teeing ground.

Definition

In teeing, the ball may be placed on the ground, on an irregularity of surface created by the player on the ground or on a tee, sand or other substance in order to raise it off the ground.

A player may stand outside the teeing ground to play a ball within it.

11-1.
Teeing

Before a player plays his first stroke with any ball from the teeing ground of the hole being played, the tee-markers are deemed to be fixed. In such circumstances, if the player moves or allows to be moved a tee-marker for the purpose of avoiding interference with his stance, the area of his intended swing or his line of play, *he shall incur the penalty for a breach of Rule 13-2.*

11-2.
Tee-Markers

If a ball, when not in play, falls off a tee or is knocked off a tee by the player in addressing it, it may be re-teed without penalty, but if a stroke is made at the ball in these circumstances, whether the ball is moving or not, the stroke counts but no penalty is incurred.

11-3.
Ball Falling Off Tee

a. MATCH PLAY
If a player, when starting a hole, plays a ball from outside the teeing ground, the opponent may immediately require the player to

11-4.
**Playing from
Outside Teeing Ground**

53

cancel the stroke so played and play a ball from within the teeing ground, without penalty.

b. STROKE PLAY

If a competitor, when starting a hole, plays a ball from outside the teeing ground, *he shall incur a penalty of two strokes* and shall then play a ball from within the teeing ground.

If the competitor plays a stroke from the next teeing ground without first correcting his mistake or, in the case of the last hole of the round, leaves the putting green without first declaring his intention to correct his mistake, *he shall be disqualified.*

Strokes played by a competitor from outside the teeing ground do not count in his score.

11-5.
Playing from Wrong Teeing Ground

The provisions of Rule 11-4 apply.

11-1. Teeing

Historical note: The wooden tee was not invented until after the turn of the century and was not commonly in use until the 1920s. Until then, balls were commonly teed on tiny pyramids of wet sand stored in buckets near each tee.

11-2. Tee-Markers

Nobody purposely tees off outside the teeing areas. When it happens, it's often because the markers have been installed carelessly so that the markers do not form a right angle to the line of play.

Vandalism is a sad fact of modern golf-course life. What to do when the markers have been removed?

If only one marker is missing, a Committee may decide to accept the scores of players who teed off from what they guessed to be the teeing ground, provided no advantage was gained. But if both markers are missing, the players may not estimate a teeing area unless there is strong evidence indicating where the markers were; e.g., depressions in the turf.

11-3. Ball Falling Off Tee

Whenever a ball falls off a tee, it behooves someone with a warped sense of humor to say, "That's one." No it isn't one, because the definition of a stroke tells us that the ball is not in play until the club moves forward and the player *intends* to strike the ball.

11-4. Playing from Outside Teeing Ground

Balls are sometimes accidentally played outside a teeing area in match play. When that happens, a delicate ethical question is raised. The opponent has every opportunity to use the Rules cruelly by requiring the shot to be replayed. That's not the way the game should be played. If I saw an opponent's ball teed ahead of the marker, I'd let him know about it and would expect him to do the same for me.

Playing from outside the teeing area in stroke play is a serious matter. It's a two stroke penalty which has to be rectified before the next hole begins. If not, the penalty is disqualification. Rectification means going back and starting anew from inside the correct teeing area.

Some other illustrations of the ramifications of Rule 11:
• Tee markers are regarded as fixed objects when playing the first

stroke from a teeing area. Thereafter, they are regarded as obstructions.

● A player whiffed his tee shot and then nervously nudged the ball off the tee before trying again. Whoops! Since the ball was in play when he attempted to hit, he incurred a penalty stroke by nudging it off the tee. The ball has to be replaced—on the tee.

● In a match played from forward teeing areas, a player inadvertently played from a back teeing area and obviously received no advantage in doing so. Nevertheless, he played from the wrong teeing ground and his opponent has the option of recalling the stroke. In stroke play, it's a two stroke penalty, and the forward teeing area must be used.

PLAYING THE BALL

SEARCHING FOR AND IDENTIFYING BALL

Definitions

A "hazard" is any <u>bunker</u> or <u>water hazard</u>.

A "bunker" is a <u>hazard</u> consisting of a prepared area of ground, often a hollow, from which turf or soil has been removed and replaced with sand or the like. Grass-covered ground bordering or within a bunker is not part of the bunker. The margin of a bunker extends vertically downwards, but not upwards.

A "water hazard" is any sea, lake, pond, river, ditch, surface drainage ditch or other open water course (whether or not containing water) and anything of a similar nature.

All ground or water within the margin of a water hazard is part of the water hazard. The margin of a water hazard extends vertically upwards and downwards. Stakes and lines defining the margins of water hazards are in the hazards.

12-1.

Searching for Ball; Seeing Ball

In searching for his ball anywhere on the course, the player may touch or bend long grass, rushes, bushes, whins, heather or the like, but only to the extent necessary to find and identify it, provided that this does not improve the lie of the ball, the area of his intended swing or his line of play.

A player is not necessarily entitled to see his ball when playing a stroke.

In a <u>hazard</u>, if a ball is covered by <u>loose impediments</u> or sand, the player may remove by probing, raking or other means as much thereof as will enable him to see a part of the ball. If an excess is removed, no penalty is incurred and the ball shall be re-covered so that only a part of the ball is visible. If the ball is moved in such removal, no penalty is incurred; the ball shall be replaced and, if

Buried in Sand

My ball is completely buried in the sand of a bunker. All I'm allowed to do is brush aside enough sand so that I can see a piece of the ball—but no more. It doesn't matter if I can't identify the ball, since there's no penalty for playing a wrong ball in a hazard. (R. 12-1)

necessary, re-covered. As to removal of loose impediments outside a hazard, see Rule 23.

If a ball lying in <u>casual water</u>, <u>ground under repair</u> or a hole, cast or runway made by a burrowing animal, a reptile or a bird is accidentally moved during search, no penalty is incurred; the ball shall be replaced, unless the player elects to proceed under Rule 25-1b.

If a ball is believed to be lying in water in a <u>water hazard</u>, the player may probe for it with a club or otherwise. If the ball is moved in so doing, no penalty is incurred; the ball shall be replaced, unless the player elects to proceed under Rule 26-1.

PENALTY FOR BREACH OF RULE 12-1:
Match play — Loss of hole; Stroke play — Two strokes.

The responsibility for playing the proper ball rests with the player. Each player should put an identification mark on his ball.
Except in a <u>hazard</u>, the player may, without penalty, lift a ball he believes to be his own for the purpose of identification and clean it to the extent necessary for identification. If the ball is the player's ball, he shall replace it. Before lifting the ball, the player must

12-2.

Identifying Ball

announce his intention to his opponent in match play or his marker or a fellow-competitor in stroke play and mark the position of the ball. He must then give his opponent, marker or fellow-competitor an opportunity to observe the lifting and replacement. If he lifts his ball without announcing his intention in advance, marking the position of the ball or giving his opponent, marker or fellow-competitor an opportunity to observe, or if he lifts his ball for identification in a hazard, or cleans it more than necessary for identification, *he shall incur a penalty of one stroke* and the ball shall be replaced.

If a player who is required to replace a ball fails to do so, *he shall incur the penalty* for a breach of Rule 20-3a, but no additional penalty under Rule 12-2 shall be applied.

12-1. Searching for Ball; Seeing Ball

A couple of key points:

● The need to identify a ball may not be used as an excuse to improve a lie. If a ball is lifted from an awkward lie, in heavy rough, it must be replaced in such a way that the stroke is just as difficult to make before the ball was lifted.

● A player who moves his ball accidentally during a search in casual water or in ground under repair is not penalized as he would be in searching for the ball through the green.

12-2. Identifying Ball

When a player wants to lift a ball because he's not sure it's his, he must say so to an opponent or fellow-competitor, and then allow the lifting and replacement to be observed. By the way, the position of the lifted ball must be marked.

A ball lifted in this circumstance may not be cleaned unless there's no other way to identify the ball, and then only enough to establish its identity.

RULE 13

BALL PLAYED AS IT LIES; LIE, AREA OF INTENDED SWING AND LINE OF PLAY; STANCE

Definitions

A "hazard" is any <u>bunker</u> or <u>water hazard</u>.

A "bunker" is a <u>hazard</u> consisting of a prepared area of ground, often a hollow, from which turf or soil has been removed and replaced with sand or the like. Grass-covered ground bordering or within a bunker is not part of the bunker. The margin of a bunker extends vertically downwards, but not upwards.

A "water hazard" is any sea, lake, pond, river, ditch, surface drainage ditch or other open water course (whether or not containing water) and anything of a similar nature.

All ground or water within the margin of a water hazard is part of the water hazard. The margin of a water hazard extends vertically upwards and downwards. Stakes and lines defining the margins of water hazards are in the hazards.

The "line of play" is the direction which the player wishes his ball to take after a stroke, plus a reasonable distance on either side of the intended direction. The line of play extends vertically upwards from the ground, but does not extend beyond the hole.

The ball shall be played as it lies, except as otherwise provided in the Rules.

(Ball at rest moved — see Rule 18.)

13-1.
Ball Played as It Lies

Except as provided in the Rules, a player shall not improve or allow to be improved:

the position or lie of his ball,

the area of his intended swing,

his line of play, or

a reasonable extension of that line beyond the hole or the area in which he is to drop or place a ball by any of the following actions:

moving, bending or breaking anything growing or fixed (including immovable obstructions and objects defining out of bounds) or removing or pressing down sand, loose soil, replaced divots, other cut turf placed in position or other irregularities of surface

except as follows:

as may occur in fairly taking his stance,

in making a stroke or the backward movement of his club for a stroke,

on the teeing ground in creating or eliminating irregularities of surface, or

13-2.
Improving Lie, Area of Intended Swing or Line of Play

Don't Improve the Lie
Here's an example of a blatant violation. The lie is being improved by pressing down behind the ball so that it sits up better. One of the underlying principles behind the Rules of Golf is that you play the ball as it lies. (R. 13-2)

59

on the <u>putting green</u> in removing sand and loose soil as provided in Rule 16-1a or in repairing damage as provided in Rule 16-1c.

The club may be grounded only lightly and shall not be pressed on the ground.

Exception: Ball lying in or touching hazard — see Rule 13-4.

13-3.

Building Stance

A player is entitled to place his feet firmly in taking his stance, but he shall not build a stance.

13-4.

Ball Lying in or Touching Hazard

Except as provided in the Rules, before making a <u>stroke</u> at a ball which lies in or touches a <u>hazard</u> (whether a <u>bunker</u> or a <u>water hazard</u>), the player shall not:

a. Test the condition of the hazard or any similar hazard,

b. Touch the ground in the hazard or water in the water hazard with a club or otherwise, or

c. Touch or move a <u>loose impediment</u> lying in or touching the hazard.

Exceptions:

1. Provided nothing is done which constitutes testing the condition of the hazard or improves the lie of the ball, there is no penalty if the player (a) touches the ground in any hazard or water in a water hazard as a result of or to prevent falling, in removing an <u>obstruction</u>, in measuring or in retrieving or lifting a ball under any Rule, or (b) places his clubs in a hazard.

2. The player after playing the stroke, or his <u>caddie</u> at any time without the authority of the player, may smooth sand or soil in the hazard, provided that, if the ball still lies in the hazard, nothing is done which improves the lie of the ball or assists the player in his subsequent play of the hole.

Note: *At any time, including at address or in the backward movement for the stroke, the player may touch with a club or otherwise any obstruction, any construction declared by the Committee to be an integral part of the course or any grass, bush, tree or other growing thing.*

PENALTY FOR BREACH OF RULE:

Match play — Loss of hole; Stroke play — Two strokes.

(Searching for ball — see Rule 12-1.)

It's my opinion that Rule 13 is violated more often than any other out of a combination of ignorance and an overpowering temptation to make the stroke just a little easier by pressing down with the clubhead.

Rule 13 is violated:

• When, during a practice swing, a branch is snapped or leaves removed *and* the next stroke is thus easier to play.

Here's the wording of an answer in a landmark decision on moving leaves:

"Whether a player who knocks down leaves with a practice swing is in breach of this Rule depends on the circumstances. In some cases, the knocking down of a number of leaves would not improve the area of the intended swing, in which case there would be no breach of the Rules. In

Touching a Hazard
After you've addressed a ball in a hazard (which happens as soon as you take a stance), the ground or water may not be touched. It's wrong to ground a club in a bunker (top) *but it's also a violation to touch a hazard* during (bottom) *the backswing.* (R. 13-4)

other cases, the knocking down of one large leaf might improve the area of the intended swing, in which case there would be a breach."

   • When a player brushes aside or lifts sand or loose soil on the apron of a putting green.

   • When a ball lies in shrubbery and the player does his bull-in-a-china shop routine by breaking, bending or moving branches that he need not have disturbed in order to take a stance.

"Fairly taking a stance" is a phrase that cries out for clarification. A Decision does so by examples of acts that are OK, including backing into a young tree or sapling, if that's the *only* way to take a fair stance, and even if

61

Grass in a Hazard
When a ball is playable in a water hazard, it's often surrounded by tall grass. In the act of addressing the ball, I'm permitted to touch the grass, but it would be a violation to ground the club. (R. 13-4)

the sapling breaks in the process; and bending or breaking the branches of a tree in order to get under the tree to play the ball. On the other hand, examples of actions which do *not* constitute fairly taking a stance are:

● Deliberately moving, bending or breaking branches to get them out of the way of a backswing or stroke.

● Standing on a branch to prevent it from interfering with the backswing or stroke.

● Hooking or braiding one branch with another for the same purpose.

● Bending with a hand a branch obscuring the ball after the stance has been taken.

As for the prohibition against "building a stance," the most famous example in the history of the game occurred in 1987 when Craig Stadler was penalized for kneeling on a towel after a viewer call-in.

I want to make two ancillary points about that incident. Odd though it seems, a Decision dealing with the same set of facts had recently been published. Accordingly, those making the Stadler ruling—the PGA Tour field staff—had no choice but to rule as they did, because a Decision carries the same weight as a Rule itself. Second, I don't believe that kneeling on a towel or jacket constitutes "building a stance." I would have voted otherwise if I were a member of the USGA Rules of Golf Committee in formulating that precedent. But so what? Everybody who plays golf would change something about the Rules. But golf, like society, needs to be a culture of law. The Rules and the Decisions can't be applied selectively.

(The Stadler case, by the way, has a fascinating "inside" story. The violation took place on Saturday but was not shown on the air. It was taped. On Sunday, the NBC producer chose to show it as an interesting or amusing happening on the preceding day. A very, very sharp viewer thought he was seeing something *live*, not on tape from a previous round. He called in thinking that Stadler should be warned so as to prevent a disqualification penalty for signing an incorrect card. Alas, the call triggered the DQ.)

As for Rule 13-4 and hazards, here are some keys:

• Remember that when your ball is in a hazard you may not move loose impediments in the hazard, and that loose impediments include stones and leaves. If you as much as touch a leaf with your backswing in a bunker, you have violated this Rule.

• On the other hand, you are entitled to set aside movable obstructions. Remember the Definition. These are man-made objects such as bottles, cigarette butts and candy wrappers.

A sprinkling of the gist of some other Rule 13 decisions:

• When sand spills over the margin of a bunker, the sand is not in the bunker.

• Ah, but your ball is on the apron when an opponent's bunker shot explodes sand in front of your ball. In that case, you may remove the sand

Ball Marks and Line of Play
You may repair a ball mark on the putting green (left) even though your ball is off the putting green. But the right to repair ball marks is strictly limited to the putting green, so you may not repair a mark on your line on an apron (right) even though you intend to putt. The apron is not part of the putting green. After making the stroke, though, you should repair the damage as part of the game's Etiquette. (R. 16-1c, 13-2)

because you are entitled to the lie you had when your ball came to rest.

• You take relief under the "embedded ball rule" in a fairway. May you repair the ball mark before you drop? No, because that would be improving the area in which you intend to drop.

• You may not remove a boundary stake that interferes with your swing.

• You are careless inside a bunker and make footprints on your line. Not being a world-class sand player, it occurs to you that you might dump your shot in one of those footprints. May you rake them? Nope.

• Your ball is just off the green, but there's casual water on the green on your line. Can you mop it up? Nope. And you can't change the position of your ball either, an option you'd have if the ball were on the green.

• Finally, a break! It's not a violation if you accidentally move loose impediments in a hazard provided that in so doing you didn't improve your situation.

• To clear up a reoccuring question, the language of Rule 13-4 now makes it clear that it's not a violation if you touch the ground in any hazard or the water in a water hazard in the act of preventing a fall provided the condition of the hazard is not tested and the lie of the ball is not improved. This was previously covered by a Decision.

RULE 14

STRIKING THE BALL

Definition

A "stroke" is the forward movement of the club made with the intention of fairly striking at and moving the ball, but if a player checks his downswing voluntarily before the clubhead reaches the ball he is deemed not to have made a stroke.

14-1.

Ball to Be Fairly Struck At

The ball shall be fairly struck at with the head of the club and must not be pushed, scraped or spooned.

14-2.

Assistance

In making a stroke, a player shall not accept physical assistance or protection from the elements.

PENALTY FOR BREACH OF RULE 14-1 OR -2:
Match play — Loss of hole; Stroke play — Two strokes.

14-3.

Artificial Devices and Unusual Equipment

If there may be any reasonable basis for doubt as to whether an item which is to be manufactured would, if used by a player during a round, cause the player to be in breach of Rule 14-3, the manufacturer should submit a sample to the United States Golf Association for a ruling, such sample to become its property for reference purposes. If a manufacturer fails to do so, he assumes the risk of an unfavorable ruling.

A player in doubt as to whether use of an item would constitute a breach of Rule 14-3 should consult the United States Golf Association.

Except as provided in the Rules, during a stipulated round the player shall not use any artificial device or unusual equipment:

a. Which might assist him in making a stroke or in his play; or

b. For the purpose of gauging or measuring distance or conditions which might affect his play; or

c. Which might assist him in gripping the club, except that plain gloves may be worn, resin, tape or gauze may be applied to the grip (provided such application does not render the grip non-conforming under Rule 4-1c) and a towel or handkerchief may be wrapped around the grip.

PENALTY FOR BREACH OF RULE 14-3: *Disqualification.*

If a player's club strikes the ball more than once in the course of a stroke, the player shall count the stroke and *add a penalty stroke,* making two strokes in all.

14-4.
Striking the Ball More than Once

A player shall not play while his ball is moving.
Exceptions:
Ball falling off tee — Rule 11-3.
Striking the ball more than once — Rule 14-4.
Ball moving in water — Rule 14-6.
When the ball begins to move only after the player has begun the stroke or the backward movement of his club for the stroke, he shall incur no penalty under this Rule for playing a moving ball, but he is not exempt from any penalty incurred under the following Rules:
Ball at rest moved by player — Rule 18-2a.
Ball at rest moving after address — Rule 18-2b.
Ball at rest moving after loose impediment touched — Rule 18-2c.

14-5.
Playing Moving Ball

When a ball is moving in water in a water hazard, the player may, without penalty, make a stroke, but he must not delay making his stroke in order to allow the wind or current to improve the position of the ball. A ball moving in water in a water hazard may be lifted if the player elects to invoke Rule 26.

PENALTY FOR BREACH OF RULE 14-5 OR -6:
Match play — Loss of hole; Stroke play — Two strokes.

14-6.
Ball Moving in Water

14-1. Ball to Be Fairly Struck At
The language in one Decision clarifies the difference between a stroke and a push. The situation was this: A player's ball was so close to a fence that when the player inserted a club behind the ball there was only half an inch between the club and the fence. Was it possible to play a stroke with such a limited backswing?

Answer: It is possible to strike a ball fairly with a half-inch backswing. However, in most cases the player would be pushing the ball, contrary to Rule 14-l. In the absence of strong evidence to the contrary, it should be ruled that the player has "pushed the ball."

14-2. Assistance
A player's caddie or partner can't shield the player in the act of making a stroke from rain or, for that matter, from the sun.

14-3. Artificial Devices and Unusual Equipment

This clause has been changed in 1992 to urge both manufacturers and players to consult with the USGA or R&A when they have any doubt as to the conformity of a device or some hunk of unusual equipment.

The best way to illustrate Rule 14-3 is to present a series of examples:
Not artificial devices. Using weighted head covers for practice swings; wearing regular eyeglasses or contact lenses; dropping a handkerchief to determine wind direction; applying gauze tape or wrapping a handkerchief around the grip to prevent slipping; using a booklet illustrating distances to the green from various landmarks; using a hand warmer.

Artificial devices. Using any of the following: field glasses which have a range-finder feature; an actual plumb line—a weight suspended from a string; a ball warmer during a round; an electronic instrument used to find balls with transmitters buried in their cores; listening to audiotapes containing instructional information.

14-4. Sriking the Ball More than Once

A well-covered disaster is a great teaching device, and so it was when T. C. Chen, cruising along with a big lead in the 1985 U.S. Open double-hit a soft pitch shot. The stroke Chen played was his third. But after the severe penalty of Rule 14-4, his next stroke was his fifth. Poor Chen emerged from the hole with an 8.

14-5. Playing a Moving Ball

One provision of this Rule is frequently misunderstood. It happens when a player addresses a ball, takes his backswing and the ball moves! The player completes his stroke and has heard that he's exempt from the restriction against playing a moving ball in this situation. Sure, that's right, but he is *not* exempt from another Rule (18-2b) which calls for a one-stroke penalty.

14-6. Ball Moving in Water

The Rules allow for playing a moving ball in water, I suppose, because it's often hard to tell if a ball in water is moving or not. The most celebrated instance of playing a ball moving in water happened before I was born, in the 1938 U.S. Open at the Cherry Hills Country Club near Denver. Pro Ray Ainsley put a shot in the creek on the 16th hole and decided the ball was playable. All told, Ainsley made 14 strokes at the ball in the hazard. Sometimes the ball was moving when he hit at it; sometimes it wasn't. He holed out in 19, the most strokes ever taken on one hole in our Open.

RULE 15

PLAYING A WRONG BALL

Definition

A "wrong ball" is any ball other than:
    a. The <u>ball in play</u>,
    b. A <u>provisional ball</u>, or
    c. In stroke play, a second ball played under Rule 3-3 or Rule 20-7b.

Note: Ball in play includes a ball substituted for the ball in play when the player is proceeding under an applicable Rule which does not permit substitution.

A player must hole out with the ball played from the teeing ground unless a Rule permits him to substitute another ball. If a player substitutes another ball when proceeding under an applicable Rule which does not permit substitution, that ball is not a wrong ball; it becomes the ball in play and, if the error is not corrected as provided in Rule 20-6, *the player shall incur a penalty of loss of hole in match play or two strokes in stroke play.*

15-1.
General

If a player plays a stroke with a wrong ball except in a hazard, *he shall lose the hole.*
If a player plays any strokes in a hazard with a wrong ball, there is no penalty. Strokes played in a hazard with a wrong ball do not count in the player's score. If the wrong ball belongs to another player, its owner shall place a ball on the spot from which the wrong ball was first played.
If the player and opponent exchange balls during the play of a hole, the first to play the wrong ball other than from a hazard shall lose the hole; when this cannot be determined, the hole shall be played out with the balls exchanged.

15-2.
Match Play

If a competitor plays a stroke or strokes with a wrong ball, *he shall incur a penalty of two strokes,* unless the only stroke or strokes played with such ball were played when it was lying in a hazard, in which case no penalty is incurred.
The competitor must correct his mistake by playing the correct ball. If he fails to correct his mistake before he plays a stroke from the next teeing ground or, in the case of the last hole of the round, fails to declare his intention to correct his mistake before leaving the putting green, *he shall be disqualified.*
Strokes played by a competitor with a wrong ball do not count in his score.
If the wrong ball belongs to another competitor, its owner shall place a ball on the spot from which the wrong ball was first played.
(Lie of ball to be placed or replaced altered — see Rule 20-3b.)

15-3.
Stroke Play

The words "wrong ball" are not the easiest to digest, even though they are clearly defined. Perhaps it's because "wrong ball" connotes a ball not belonging to the player. Actually, if you put a ball in play; e.g., drive from the tee, with someone else's ball, that is not a wrong ball. Let's walk through the three provisions of Rule 15.

15-1. General
You are not allowed to substitute balls during a hole unless you can find a specific authorization to do so in the Rules. This, for example, stops the introduction of what some golfers like to call "putting balls," a shiny new one put in place of a battered veteran used to get over a body of water.

15-2. Match Play

Simple enough: As soon as a player plays a wrong ball, except in a hazard, he loses the hole. In four-ball play the erring partner is disqualified from that hole only, but there's no penalty for the partner.

15-3. Stroke Play

This is where it gets sticky. When a competitor plays a wrong ball, he immediately incurs a two-stroke penalty and does not count any more strokes played with the wrong ball. But the mistake *must* be rectified. That means returning to play the correct ball before teeing off on the next hole or, if the mistake is made on the last hole, before he leaves the putting green. The penalty for failing to rectify: disqualification.

Some Rule 15 Decisions to chew on:
• A player swings at a ball, not his, and misses.
Answer: the player played a stroke (remember intent) at a wrong ball.
• After the sixth hole, a player realizes he's not playing the ball with which he started the round. The player has no idea when he first played the ball in his hand. This is when a Committee earns its keep. It should tilt in the player's direction by ruling no penalty if this strange ball might have been put into play at the start of any hole. But *if* the Committee becomes satisifed that the transfer took place during play of a hole, it's a wrong-ball situation.

The outcomes:
Stroke play—The player is disqualified *unless* the determination is that the exchange took place during the sixth hole, in which case rectification is still possible since the player has not yet teed off on the seventh hole.
Match play—If it's not possible to determine where the violation took place, the player should be penalized the loss of one hole he has won. If he hasn't yet lost a hole, change a halved hole to a loss. If he has lost all six holes, the worst has already happened to him.

THE PUTTING GREEN

THE PUTTING GREEN

Definitions

The "putting green" is all ground of the hole being played which is specially prepared for putting or otherwise defined as such by the Committee. A ball is on the putting green when any part of it touches the putting green.

The "line of putt" is the line which the player wishes his ball to take after a stroke on the <u>putting green</u>. Except with respect to Rule 16-1e, the line of putt includes a reasonable distance on either side of the intended line. The line of putt does not extend beyond the hole.

A ball is "holed" when it is at rest within the circumference of the hole and all of it is below the level of the lip of the hole.

16-1.
General

a. TOUCHING LINE OF PUTT

The <u>line of putt</u> must not be touched except:

(i) the player may move sand and loose soil on the putting green and other <u>loose impediments</u> by picking them up or by brushing them aside with his hand or a club without pressing anything down;

(ii) in addressing the ball, the player may place the club in front of the ball without pressing anything down;

(iii) in measuring — Rule 10-4;

(iv) in lifting the ball — Rule 16-1b;

(v) in pressing down a ball-marker;

(vi) in repairing old hole plugs or ball marks on the putting green — Rule 16-1c; and

(vii) in removing movable <u>obstructions</u> — Rule 24-1.

(Indicating line for putting on putting green — see Rule 8-2b.)

Don't Repair Spike Marks

The line of putt is sacrosanct. It is not to be improved unless the rules specify exceptions—for example, repairing ball marks and removing loose impediments. This most assuredly means that irregularities on the line of putt, such as raised tufts of grass, may not be tamped down, as is being done here. (R. 16-1a)

Don't Use a Hat as a Brush

You are allowed to pick up or brush aside loose impediments on the line of putt. But all you can use are your hands or a club. If anything else is used—a hat, for instance—it is a violation. (R. 16-1a)

Repairing Ball Marks

Ball marks on putting greens may be repaired, even if they're on your line. As a matter of fact, they should be repaired, no matter where they are. I use a tee to loosen the soil around the mark. After the compacted soil has been loosened at several positions, I pull the turf toward the center of the damaged spot. The smoothing process can be done either with a putter, one's hand, or by stepping down on the spot. (R. 16-1c)

b. LIFTING BALL

A ball on the <u>putting green</u> may be lifted and, if desired, cleaned. A ball so lifted shall be replaced on the spot from which it was lifted.

c. REPAIR OF HOLE PLUGS, BALL MARKS AND OTHER DAMAGE

The player may repair an old hole plug or damage to the <u>putting green</u> caused by the impact of a ball, whether or not the player's ball lies on the putting green. If the ball is moved in the process of such repair, it shall be replaced, without penalty. Any other damage to the putting green shall not be repaired if it might assist the player in his subsequent play of the hole.

d. TESTING SURFACE

During the play of a hole, a player shall not test the surface of the <u>putting green</u> by rolling a ball or roughening or scraping the surface.

e. STANDING ASTRIDE OR ON LINE OF PUTT

The player shall not make a <u>stroke</u> on the <u>putting green</u> from a <u>stance</u> astride, or with either foot touching, the line of putt or an extension of that line behind the ball.

f. POSITION OF CADDIE OR PARTNER

While making a <u>stroke</u> on the putting green, the player shall not allow his caddie, his partner or his partner's caddie to position himself on or close to an extension of the line of putt behind the ball.

g. PLAYING STROKE WHILE ANOTHER BALL IN MOTION

The player shall not play a stroke while another ball is in motion after a stroke from the putting green, except that, if a player does so, he incurs no penalty if it was his turn to play.

(Lifting ball interfering with or assisting play while another ball in motion — see Rule 22.)

PENALTY FOR BREACH OF RULE 16-1:
Match play — Loss of hole; Stroke play — Two strokes.

16-2.
Ball Overhanging Hole

When any part of the ball overhangs the lip of the hole, the player is allowed enough time to reach the hole without unreasonable delay and an additional ten seconds to determine whether the ball is at rest. If by then the ball has not fallen into the hole, it is deemed to be at rest. If the ball subsequently falls into the hole, the player is deemed to have holed out with his last stroke, and *he shall add a penalty stroke to his score* for the hole; otherwise there is no penalty under this Rule.

(Undue delay — see Rule 6-7.)

The USGA says that, depending on one's ability, 30 to 40 percent of all strokes played are played on the putting greens. That applies to me and to high-handicap golfers. It's only natural that a disproportionate number of Rules incidents occur on putting greens, where all players and balls eventually converge.

16-1a. Touching the Line of Putt

The line of putt is holy ground except during the seven acts (go back and look at them) listed in this Rule. Here are some common transgressions:

● Repairing spike or scuff marks. Many golfers think the Rule should be liberalized in this regard. I don't. It would be next to impossible to define or agree on the difference between damage caused by a spike and regular damage caused by the traffic of feet. Easing up on the Rule would also make the game slower. That's the last thing we need.

• Brushing aside or sopping up casual water on the line of putt. The same applies to dew.

• Walking or stepping on your line of putt if it somehow improves the line. A Decision says there is no violation if the line is not improved and the line was stepped on accidentally.

• Brushing away leaves with a hat or towel. The Rule limits you to using your hand or a club.

16-1b. Lifting Ball

I'm afraid the average golfer lifts his ball all too often—perhaps in emulation of what he sees on television. That's just one of the reasons golf on the Tour is too slow. By the way, you are not allowed to rotate the position of a ball in order to line up its marking just so, without first marking its position.

16-1c. Repair of Hole Plugs, Ball Marks and Other Damage

I wish there was a way and means to penalize every golfer who fails to repair ball marks, whether on his line of putt or not. A golfer should step on a green with a built-in self-operating scanner, looking for ball marks to repair.

16-1d. Testing Surface

If I could rub the surface of greens, it would help me to "read" the grain better and make putting just a little easier. Interpretations of what constitutes testing in this context tilt in the direction of the player. For instance, a player who rolls a ball after conceding a putt is not in violation unless it's determined he did so to test the surface.

16-1e. Standing Astride or on Line of Putt

This clause bans what used to be called "straddle" putting, a variation popularized by Sam Snead. Sam's reaction to the ban was to continue to putt croquet style, but to stand with both feet together *off* the line of putt.

16-1f. Position of Caddie or Partner

Johnny Miller, when he began to lose confidence in his putting, had his caddie crouch behind him on the green to give counsel on alignment. That practice was stopped with the argument that the practice was making the caddie more than he should be. The prohibition applies to partners as well as caddies.

Interestingly, some players on the Ladies PGA Tour have positioned their caddies behind them during shots played in the fairways—among them Betsy King and Julie Inkster. That's not a violation since Rule 16-1f applies only to putting green actions.

16-1g. Playing Stroke While Another Ball in Motion

An easy one. No one plays or touches his ball while another ball is in motion. There's a 1992 modification: If the player whose turn it was to play, putts only to see that another player has played out of turn, and both balls are in motion, the player whose turn it was to play is not penalized.

Direction for Putting
My caddie or my partner can use the flagstick to point (top) to the line of putt. But if he touches (bottom) the putting green to indicate the line, I'm penalized. (R. 8-2)

16-2. Ball Overhanging Hole

There was a great to-do on television at the 1991 Masters, when Ian Woosnam, with whom I was paired, had a putt overhang the hole on the 15th. Ian, realizing his time was up, was prepared to hole out, but he expressed concern that as he was pulling out the flagstick the ball might fall in simultaneously, strike the flagstick and cause him a penalty. I suggested to him, "Mark it," meaning he could mark and lift the ball and then haul out the flagstick without concern. My words were misinterpreted as being a warning to him that he was taking too long. Nothing of the kind.

A vivid illustration of the working of Rule 16-2 happened on the European Tour in 1990. Ryder Cup player Sam Torrance had a ball overhang the edge of the hole. He waited 27 seconds, as determined by a review of a television tape. The ball then fell in. Sam raised his arms in triumph, thinking he'd made a 3. Wrong! He'd made a 4, because he waited longer than ten seconds.

The lesson is this: After waiting ten seconds at the hole, there's no point in waiting any longer. Even if the ball falls in, it will not affect your score.

RULE 17

THE FLAGSTICK

17-1.

Flagstick Attended, Removed or Held Up

Before and during the stroke, the player may have the flagstick attended, removed or held up to indicate the position of the hole. This may be done only on the authority of the player before he plays his stroke.

If, prior to the stroke, the flagstick is attended, removed or held up by anyone with the player's knowledge and no objection is made, the player shall be deemed to have authorized it. If anyone attends or holds up the flagstick or stands near the hole while a stroke is being played, he shall be deemed to be attending the flagstick until the ball comes to rest.

17-2.

Unauthorized Attendance

a. MATCH PLAY

In match play, an opponent or his caddie shall not, without the authority or prior knowledge of the player, attend, remove or hold up the flagstick while the player is making a stroke or his ball is in motion.

b. STROKE PLAY

In stroke play, if a fellow-competitor or his caddie attends, removes or holds up the flagstick without the competitor's authority or prior knowledge while the competitor is making a stroke or his ball is in motion, *the fellow-competitor shall incur the penalty* for breach of this Rule. In such circumstances, if the competitor's ball strikes the flagstick, the person attending it or anything carried by him, the competitor incurs no penalty and the ball shall be played as it lies, except that, if the stroke was played from the putting green, the stroke shall be cancelled, the ball replaced and the stroke replayed.

PENALTY FOR BREACH OF RULE 17-1 OR -2:
Match play — Loss of hole; Stroke play — Two strokes.

Flagstick Held Aloft

When a green is elevated, it isn't always possible to see the flagstick when you address the ball. In that case, the flagstick may be held up at the hole (1), and it can be attended in that manner during the stroke. But if the flagstick is held aloft away from the hole (2), the caddie has to get off the line before the stroke is played. (R. 17-1)

17-3.
Ball Striking Flagstick or Attendant

The player's ball shall not strike:

a. The flagstick when attended, removed or held up by the player, his partner or either of their caddies, or by another person with the player's authority or prior knowledge; or

b. The player's caddie, his partner or his partner's caddie when attending the flagstick, or another person attending the flagstick with the player's authority or prior knowledge or anything carried by any such person; or

c. The flagstick in the hole, unattended, when the ball has been played from the <u>putting green</u>.

PENALTY FOR BREACH OF RULE 17-3:
Match play — Loss of hole; Stroke play — Two strokes, and the ball shall be played as it lies.

Striking the Flagstick

When I putt from off the green, I may prefer to have the flagstick remain in the hole, since there's no penalty for striking the flagstick from off the green. But when the ball is played from on the green, there is a penalty for striking the flagstick, which should either be attended or set aside. (R. 17-3)

If the ball rests against the flagstick when it is in the hole, the player or another person authorized by him may move or remove the flagstick and if the ball falls into the hole, the player shall be deemed to have holed out with his last stroke; otherwise, the ball, if <u>moved</u>, shall be placed on the lip of the hole, without penalty.

17-4.

Ball Resting Against Flagstick

The flagstick is there as an indicator of where the hole is. Its incidental use as a backstop has been the cause of many a controversy and many changes in the flagstick Rule over the years. Happily, the Rule has comfortably settled into a form we can all readily understand:

● If your ball is *on* the putting green and your ball then strikes the flagstick, whether attended or unattended, the penalty is loss of hole in match play or the customary two strokes in stroke play.

● If your ball is *off* the putting green, you may try to use the flagstick as a backstop. No penalty for hitting it, so long as you did not authorize someone to attend it.

BALL MOVED, DEFLECTED OR STOPPED

BALL AT REST MOVED

Definitions

A ball is deemed to have "moved" if it leaves its position and comes to rest in any other place.

An "outside agency" is any agency not part of the match or, in stroke play, not part of the competitor's side, and includes a referee, a marker, an observer or a forecaddie. Neither wind nor water is an outside agency.

"Equipment" is anything used, worn or carried by or for the player except any ball he has played at the hole being played and any small object, such as a coin or a tee, when used to mark the position of a ball or the extent of an area in which a ball is to be dropped. Equipment includes a golf cart, whether or not motorized. If such a cart is shared by two or more players, the cart and everything in it are deemed to be the equipment of the player whose ball is involved except that, when the cart is being moved by one of the players sharing it, the cart and everything in it are deemed to be that player's equipment.

Note: *A ball played at the hole being played is equipment when it has been lifted and not put back into play.*

A player has "addressed the ball" when he has taken his stance and has also grounded his club, except that in a hazard a player has addressed the ball when he has taken his stance.

Taking the "stance" consists in a player placing his feet in position for and preparatory to making a stroke.

18-1.
By Outside Agency

If a ball at rest is moved by an outside agency, the player shall incur no penalty and the ball shall be replaced before the player plays another stroke.

(Player's ball at rest moved by another ball — see Rule 18-5.)

a. GENERAL

When a player's ball is <u>in play</u>, if:

(i) the player, his partner or either of their caddies lifts or moves it, touches it purposely (except with a club in the act of addressing it) or causes it to move except as permitted by a Rule, or

(ii) equipment of the player or his partner causes the ball to move,

the player shall incur a penalty stroke. The ball shall be replaced unless the movement of the ball occurs after the player has begun his swing and he does not discontinue his swing.

Under the Rules no penalty is incurred if a player accidentally causes his ball to move in the following circumstances:

In measuring to determine which ball farther from hole — Rule 10-4

In searching for covered ball in hazard or for ball in <u>casual water</u>, <u>ground under repair</u>, etc. — Rule 12-1

In the process of repairing hole plug or ball mark — Rule 16-1c

In the process of removing <u>loose impediment</u> on <u>putting green</u> — Rule 18-2c

18-2.

By Player, Partner, Caddie or Equipment

Stop that Outside Agency!
The player is Johnny Bulla; the scene, the 1950 U.S. Open Championship at the Merion Golf Club. An outside agency snatched Bulla's ball and made a clean getaway. Whenever an outside agency—be it human, animal or mechanical—moves a ball, the ball is to be replaced without penalty. If the outside agency is a successful thief, another ball may be substituted. (R. 18-1)

In the process of lifting ball under a Rule — Rule 20-1

In the process of placing or replacing ball under a Rule — Rule 20-3a

In complying with Rule 22 relating to lifting ball interfering with or assisting play

In removal of movable <u>obstruction</u> — Rule 24-1.

b. BALL MOVING AFTER ADDRESS

If a player's <u>ball in play moves</u> after he has <u>addressed</u> it (other than as a result of a stroke), the player shall be deemed to have moved the ball and *shall incur a penalty stroke*. The player shall replace the ball unless the movement of the ball occurs after he has begun his swing and he does not discontinue his swing.

c. BALL MOVING AFTER LOOSE IMPEDIMENT TOUCHED

<u>Through the green</u>, if the ball <u>moves</u> after any <u>loose impediment</u> lying within a club-length of it has been touched by the player, his partner or either of their caddies and before the player has <u>addressed</u> it, the player shall be deemed to have moved the ball and *shall incur a penalty stroke*. The player shall replace the ball unless the movement of the ball occurs after he has begun his swing and he does not discontinue his swing.

On the <u>putting green</u>, if the ball or the ball-marker <u>moves</u> in the process of removing any <u>loose impediment</u>, the ball or the ball-marker shall be replaced. There is no penalty provided the movement of the ball or the ball-marker is directly attributable to the removal of the loose impediment. Otherwise, *the player shall incur a penalty stroke* under Rule 18-2a or 20-1.

18-3.

By Opponent, Caddie or Equipment in Match Play

a. DURING SEARCH

If, during search for a player's ball, it is moved by an opponent, his caddie or his <u>equipment</u>, no penalty is incurred and the player shall replace the ball.

b. OTHER THAN DURING SEARCH

If, other than during search for a ball, the ball is touched or moved by an opponent, his caddie or his <u>equipment</u>, except as otherwise provided in the Rules, *the opponent shall incur a penalty stroke*. The player shall replace the ball.

(Ball moved in measuring to determine which ball farther from the hole — see Rule 10-4.)

(Playing a wrong ball — see Rule 15-2.)

(Ball moved in complying with Rule 22 relating to lifting ball interfering with or assisting play.)

18-4.

By Fellow-Competitor, Caddie or Equipment in Stroke Play

If a competitor's ball is moved by a fellow-competitor, his caddie or his <u>equipment</u>, no penalty is incurred. The competitor shall replace his ball.

(Playing a wrong ball — see Rule 15-3.)

18-5.

By Another Ball

If a ball in play and at rest is moved by another ball in motion after a stroke, the moved ball shall be replaced.

*PENALTY FOR BREACH OF RULE:

Match play — Loss of hole; Stroke play — Two strokes.

If a player who is required to replace a ball fails to do so, he

*shall incur the general penalty for breach of Rule 18 but no addi-
tional penalty under Rule 18 shall be applied.*

> ***Note 1:*** *If a ball to be replaced under this Rule is not immediate-
ly recoverable, another ball may be substituted.*

> ***Note 2:*** *If it is impossible to determine the spot on which a ball is
to be placed, see Rule 20-3c.*

Rule 18 takes us through the tangle of possibilities that occur when a
ball at rest is moved.

18-1. By Outside Agency

Whether your ball is moved by another golfer playing another hole, or by
a ball-loving dog, it's been moved by that breed known as an outside
agency. You must replace the ball. It will often happen that you will not
know the spot from which it was moved. In that case, according to Rule 20-
3c, you drop a ball as near as possible to where the ball lay, not nearer the
hole. There's one exception: If the ball was moved from a putting green, it is
to be placed, not dropped, whether or not its precise resting place was
known.

18-2. By Player, Partner, Caddie or Equipment

Red flag warning: If you so much as reach down and touch your ball,
even without moving it, without cause under the Rules, there is a penalty
stroke. The onus is on you to know whether or not the Rules give you
license whenever you want to lift your ball.

There are instances (in fact, eight of them listed in this clause) when the
accidental moving of your ball is not in violation of the Rules.

Focus on the word "equipment" and its definition. Be mindful that a golf
cart is part of the player's equipment. When a player runs over his ball
while driving a cart, he has violated Rule 18.

Again, we encounter one of the code's favorite words "deemed." Once
you've addressed a ball and it moves, you are "deemed" to be the cause.
When it's very windy or my ball is perched precariously, I often take the
precaution of not grounding my club and have therefore not addressed it.
That can save a stroke.

"Deemed" pops up again in Clause c. If you move a loose impediment
within one club-length of your ball and the ball subsequently moves, don't
bother arguing that something other than the removal of the loose impediment caused the ball to move.

One of the game's most perplexing situations occurs when the player
has addressed a ball, takes a backswing and the ball moves. That's a one-
stroke penalty and the ball must be replaced if the player stops before
making a stroke. But if the stroke is made—even as the ball is moving, the
stroke counts, add a penalty stroke because the ball moved, and the ball is
played as it then lies.

18-3. By Opponent, Caddie or Equipment in Match Play

If an opponent accidentally moves your ball while he's being good
enough to assist in the search, there's no penalty. In any other circumstance, when a ball is moved by an opponent, there is one penalty stroke.
Remember, in every case the ball must be replaced.

81

18-4. By Fellow-Competitor, Caddie or Equipment in Stroke Play

Since we're into stroke play, the proper term becomes "fellow-competitor" who is neither your partner nor your opponent. In stroke play, he's an outside agency. Thus, he is not penalized for moving your ball whether or not in a search.

18-5. By Another Ball

Many of us grew up with a Rules provision that in match play gave an option to the player whose ball was moved by another ball. That option was removed in 1984. The ball is to be replaced.

RULE 19

BALL IN MOTION DEFLECTED OR STOPPED

Definitions

An "outside agency" is any agency not part of the match or, in stroke play, not part of the competitor's side, and includes a referee, a marker, an observer or a forecaddie. Neither wind nor water is an outside agency.

"Equipment" is anything used, worn or carried by or for the player except any ball he has played at the hole being played and any small object, such as a coin or a tee, when used to mark the position of a ball or the extent of an area in which a ball is to be dropped. Equipment includes a golf cart, whether or not motorized. If such a cart is shared by two or more players, the cart and everything in it are deemed to be the equipment of the player whose ball is involved except that, when the cart is being moved by one of the players sharing it, the cart and everything in it are deemed to be that player's equipment.

Note: *A ball played at the hole being played is equipment when it has been lifted and not put back into play.*

19-1.
By Outside Agency

If a ball in motion is accidentally deflected or stopped by any outside agency, it is a rub of the green, no penalty is incurred and the ball shall be played as it lies except:

a. If a ball in motion after a stroke other than on the putting green comes to rest in or on any moving or animate outside agency, the player shall, through the green or in a hazard, drop the ball, or on the putting green place the ball, as near as possible to the spot where the outside agency was when the ball came to rest in or on it, and

b. If a ball in motion after a stroke on the putting green is deflected or stopped by, or comes to rest in or on, any moving or animate outside agency except a worm or an insect, the stroke shall be cancelled, the ball replaced and the stroke replayed.

If the ball is not immediately recoverable, another ball may be substituted.

(Player's ball deflected or stopped by another ball — see Rule 19-5.)

Note: If the referee or the Committee determines that a player's ball has been purposely deflected or stopped by an <u>outside agency</u>, Rule 1-4 applies to the player. If the outside agency is a fellow-competitor or his caddie, Rule 1-2 applies to the fellow-competitor.

a. MATCH PLAY

If a player's ball is accidentally deflected or stopped by himself, his partner or either of their caddies or <u>equipment</u>, *he shall lose the hole.*

b. STROKE PLAY

If a competitor's ball is accidentally deflected or stopped by himself, his partner or either of their caddies or <u>equipment</u>, *the competitor shall incur a penalty of two strokes.* The ball shall be played as it lies, except when it comes to rest in or on the competitor's, his partner's or either of their caddies' clothes or equipment, in which case the competitor shall <u>through the green</u> or in a <u>hazard</u> drop the ball, or on the <u>putting green</u> place the ball, as near as possible to where the article was when the ball came to rest in or on it.

Exception: Dropped ball — see Rule 20-2a.

(Ball purposely deflected or stopped by player, partner or caddie — see Rule 1-2.)

19-2.

By Player, Partner, Caddie or Equipment

If a player's ball is accidentally deflected or stopped by an opponent, his caddie or his <u>equipment</u>, no penalty is incurred. The player may play the ball as it lies or, before another <u>stroke</u> is played by either side, cancel the stroke and play a ball without penalty as nearly as possible at the spot from which the original ball was last played (see Rule 20-5).

If the ball has come to rest in or on the opponent's or his caddie's clothes or equipment, the player may <u>through the green</u> or in a <u>hazard</u> drop the ball, or on the <u>putting green</u> place the ball, as near as possible to where the article was when the ball came to rest in or on it.

Exception: Ball striking person attending flagstick — see Rule 17-3b.

(Ball purposely deflected or stopped by opponent or caddie — see Rule 1-2.)

19-3.

By Opponent, Caddie or Equipment in Match Play

See Rule 19-1 regarding ball deflected by outside agency.

19-4.

By Fellow-Competitor, Caddie or Equipment in Stroke Play

If a player's ball in motion after a stroke is deflected or stopped by a ball at rest, the player shall play his ball as it lies. In stroke play, if both balls lay on the <u>putting green</u> prior to the stroke, *the player incurs a penalty of two strokes.* Otherwise, no penalty is incurred.

If a player's ball in motion after a stroke is deflected or stopped by another ball in motion, the player shall play his ball as it lies. There is no penalty unless the player was in breach of Rule 16-1g, in which case *he shall incur the penalty for breach of that Rule.*

19-5.

By Another Ball

83

Exception: Ball in motion after a stroke on the putting green deflected or stopped by moving or animate outside agency — see Rule 19-1b.

PENALTY FOR BREACH OF RULE:
Match play — Loss of hole; Stroke play — Two strokes.

In considering Rule 18, we moved through the tangle of what to do when a ball *at rest* is moved. Rule 19 moves on to reacting when a ball *in motion* is accidentally stopped or deflected. We dealt with purposeful deflections way back in Rule 1-2.

19-1. By Outside Agency

The phrase "rub of the green" crossed over from golf into everyday usage where it's taken to mean a bit of bad luck. But in golf "rub of the green" can cut either way. If a ball bounces out of bounds after colliding with a piece of maintainence equipment, that's one "rub of the green"; but if your ball was headed toward out of bounds, and that same piece of equipment deflects the ball so that it stays in bounds, that, too, is a "rub of the green."

19-2. By Player, Partner, Caddie or Equipment

The general penalties apply. In match play, it's loss of hole when a moving ball is deflected by the player, his partner, caddie or equipment. In stroke play, it's two strokes and the ball is played as it then lies.

The Rules are necessarily dotted with Exceptions. We find an example here. You already know that a ball is in play once it's dropped, so you'd be inclined to think that if a ball is dropped and then strikes your foot there's a penalty. Good thinking, except that there's an Exception after 19-2 which directs you over to the Rule governing dropping where you'll be told there's no penalty when a ball strikes the player or his equipment after a drop. The ball has to be dropped again.

19-3. By Opponent, Caddie or Equipment in Match Play

Assuming the deflection is an accident, there's no penalty when a ball is deflected by an opponent. The owner of the ball then has a choice. He can either play the ball as it lies or opt to cancel the stroke and play it over.

19-4. By Fellow Competitor, Caddie or Equipment in Stroke Play

It's the same as in Rule 19-1. There is no penalty for accidental deflections in stroke play.

19-5. By a Ball at Rest

With one glaring exception, there is no penalty when a moving ball is deflected by a ball at rest. That exception occurs only in stroke play when both balls were on the putting green before the stroke was played. In that case, the player whose ball did the deflecting (not the owner of the ball that was deflected) suffers a two-stroke penalty. He plays his ball as it lies. If the other ball was moved, its owner must replace it.

RELIEF SITUATIONS AND PROCEDURE

RULE 20

LIFTING, DROPPING AND PLACING; PLAYING FROM WRONG PLACE

A ball to be lifted under the Rules may be lifted by the player, his partner or another person authorized by the player. In any such case, the player shall be responsible for any breach of the Rules.

The position of the ball shall be marked before it is lifted under a Rule which requires it to be replaced. If it is not marked, *the player shall incur a penalty of one stroke* and the ball shall be replaced. If it is not replaced, *the player shall incur the general penalty* for breach of this Rule but no additional penalty under Rule 20-1 shall be applied.

If a ball or the ball-marker is accidentally moved in the process of lifting the ball under a Rule or marking its position, the ball or the ball-marker shall be replaced. There is no penalty provided the movement of the ball or the ball-marker is directly attributable to the specific act of marking the position of or lifting the ball. Otherwise, *the player shall incur a penalty stroke* under this Rule or Rule 18-2a.

Exception: If a player incurs a penalty for failing to act in accordance with Rule 5-3 or 12-2, no additional penalty under Rule 20-1 shall be applied.

Note: *The position of a ball to be lifted should be marked by placing a ball-marker, a small coin or other similar object immediately behind the ball. If the ball-marker interferes with the play,* <u>stance</u> *or* <u>stroke</u> *of another player, it should be placed one or or more clubhead-lengths to one side.*

a. By Whom and How
A ball to be dropped under the Rules shall be dropped by the

20-1.
Lifting

20-2.
Dropping and Re-dropping

How to Drop
The dropping procedure is simple. Extend your arm horizontally and drop the ball. You can do it to the side, as I'm doing, or directly in front of you. (R. 20-2a)

player himself. He shall stand erect, hold the ball at shoulder height and arm's length and drop it. If a ball is dropped by any other person or in any other manner and the error is not corrected as provided in Rule 20-6, *the player shall incur a penalty stroke.*

If the ball touches the player, his partner, either of their caddies or their equipment before or after it strikes a part of the course, the ball shall be re-dropped, without penalty. There is no limit to the number of times a ball shall be re-dropped in such circumstances.

Geometry of Ball Dropping

Here's a common drop situation. The ball lies in ground under repair at X. First the player determines the nearest point of relief, which in this illustration is at Y—just outside the ground-under-repair area.

The player must drop within one club-length of Y, but he can't drop in the shaded area because all of that area is either closer to the hole or within ground under repair.

That leaves him with the white area. The ball remains in play if it's dropped at Point A even though it rolls outside the circle to Point B—which is less than two club-lengths from A. (R. 25-1b)

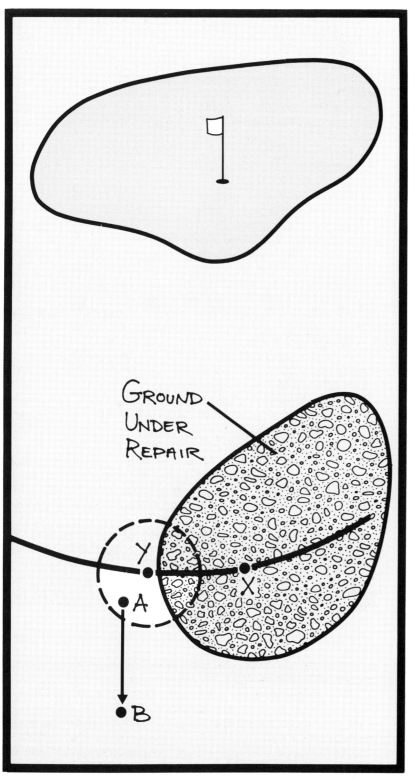

GROUND UNDER REPAIR

(Taking action to influence position or movement of ball — see Rule 1-2.)

b. WHERE TO DROP

When a ball is to be dropped as near as possible to a specific spot, it shall be dropped not nearer the hole than the specific spot which, if it is not precisely known to the player, shall be estimated.

A ball when dropped must first strike a part of the course where the applicable Rule requires it to be dropped. If it is not so dropped, Rules 20-6 and -7 apply.

c. WHEN TO RE-DROP

A dropped ball shall be re-dropped without penalty if it:

(i) rolls into a hazard;

(ii) rolls out of a hazard;

(iii) rolls onto a putting green;

(iv) rolls out of bounds;

(v) rolls to a position where there is interference by the condition from which relief was taken under Rule 24-2 (immovable obstruction) or Rule 25-1 (abnormal ground condition);

(vi) rolls and comes to rest more than two club-lengths from where it first struck a part of the course; or

(vii) rolls and comes to rest nearer the hole than its original position or estimated position (see Rule 20-2b) unless otherwise permitted by the Rules.

If the ball when re-dropped rolls into any position listed above, it shall be placed as near as possible to the spot where it first struck a part of the course when re-dropped.

If a ball to be re-dropped or placed under this Rule is not immediately recoverable, another ball may be substituted.

20-3.
Placing and Replacing

a. BY WHOM AND WHERE

A ball to be placed under the Rules shall be placed by the player or his partner. If a ball is to be replaced, the player, his partner or the person who lifted or moved it shall place it on the spot from which it was lifted or moved. In any such case, the player shall be responsible for any breach of the Rules.

If a ball or the ball-marker is accidentally moved in the process of placing or replacing the ball, the ball or the ball-marker shall be replaced. There is no penalty provided the movement of the ball or the ball-marker is directly attributable to the specific act of placing or replacing the ball or removing the ball-marker. Otherwise, the player shall incur a penalty stroke under Rule 18-2a or 20-1.

b. LIE OF BALL TO BE PLACED OR REPLACED ALTERED

If the original lie of a ball to be placed or replaced has been altered:

(i) except in a hazard, the ball shall be placed in the nearest lie most similar to the original lie which is not more than one club-length from the original lie, not nearer the hole and not in a hazard;

(ii) in a water hazard, the ball shall be placed in accordance with Clause (i) above, except that the ball must be placed in the water hazard;

(iii) in a bunker, the original lie shall be re-created as nearly as possible and the ball shall be placed in that lie.

c. Spot Not Determinable

If it is impossible to determine the spot where the ball is to be placed or replaced:

(i) <u>through the green</u>, the ball shall be dropped as near as possible to the place where it lay but not in a <u>hazard</u>;

(ii) in a hazard, the ball shall be dropped in the hazard as near as possible to the place where it lay;

(iii) on the <u>putting green</u>, the ball shall be placed as near as possible to the place where it lay but not in a hazard.

d. Ball Fails to Remain on Spot

If a ball when placed fails to remain on the spot on which it was placed, it shall be replaced without penalty. If it still fails to remain on that spot:

(i) except in a <u>hazard</u>, it shall be placed at the nearest spot not nearer the hole or in a hazard where it can be placed at rest;

(ii) in a hazard, it shall be placed in the hazard at the nearest spot not nearer the hole where it can be placed at rest.

PENALTY FOR BREACH OF RULE 20-1, -2 OR -3:
Match play — Loss of hole; Stroke play — Two strokes.

20-4.
When Ball Dropped or Placed Is in Play

If the player's <u>ball in play</u> has been lifted, it is again in play when dropped or placed.

A substituted ball becomes the ball in play if it is dropped or placed under an applicable Rule, whether or not such Rule permits substitution. A ball substituted under an inapplicable Rule is a <u>wrong ball</u>.

20-5.
Playing Next Stroke from Where Previous Stroke Played

When, under the Rules, a player elects or is required to play his next <u>stroke</u> from where a previous stroke was played, he shall proceed as follows: If the stroke is to be played from the <u>teeing ground</u>, the ball to be played shall be played from anywhere within the teeing ground and may be teed; if the stroke is to be played from <u>through the green</u> or a <u>hazard</u>, it shall be dropped; if the stroke is to be played on the <u>putting green</u>, it shall be placed.

PENALTY FOR BREACH OF RULE 20-5:
Match play — Loss of hole; Stroke play — Two strokes.

20-6.
Lifting Ball Wrongly Dropped or Placed

A ball dropped or placed in a wrong place or otherwise not in accordance with the Rules but not played may be lifted, without penalty, and the player shall then proceed correctly.

20-7.
Playing from Wrong Place

For a ball played from outside the teeing ground or from a wrong teeing ground — see Rule 11-4 and -5.

a. Match Play

If a player plays a stroke with a ball which has been dropped or placed in a wrong place, *he shall lose the hole.*

b. Stroke Play

If a competitor plays a stroke with (i) his original ball which has been dropped or placed in a wrong place, (ii) a substituted ball which has been dropped or placed under an applicable Rule but in a wrong place, or (iii) his ball in play when it has been moved and not replaced in a case where the Rules require replacement, *he shall,* provided a serious breach has not occurred, *incur the penalty*

89

prescribed by the applicable Rule and play out the hole with the ball.

If, after playing from a wrong place, a competitor becomes aware of that fact and believes that a serious breach may be involved, he may, provided he has not played a stroke from the next teeing ground or, in the case of the last hole of the round, left the putting green, declare that he will play out the hole with a second ball dropped or placed in accordance with the Rules. The competitor shall report the facts to the Committee before returning his score card; if he fails to do so, *he shall be disqualified.* The Committee shall determine whether a serious breach of the Rule occurred. If so, the score with the second ball shall count and *the competitor shall add two penalty strokes to his score with that ball.*

If a serious breach has occurred and the competitor has failed to correct it as prescribed above, *he shall be disqualified.*

Note: *If a competitor plays a second ball, penalty strokes incurred by playing the ball ruled not to count and strokes subsequently taken with that ball shall be disregarded.*

20-1. Lifting

Students: Don't pick up the ball unless you know what you are going to do with it.

First, be certain the Rules allow you to lift it. Second, you must know whether the ball is to be dropped or placed when it is put back in play. (If it's to be replaced, you must mark its position before lifting.)

When the procedure calls for a drop, you must know *where* to drop.

There are five possibilities: (1) as near as possible to the spot from which it was lifted, as when a ball is embedded in a fairway; (2) within one club-length of the nearest point of relief; e.g., from ground under repair; (3) within two club-lengths of the relief point; e.g., from a lateral water hazard; (4) dropping anywhere along a line, as happens when relief is taken from a water hazard; or (5) as near as possible to the spot where it was last played; e.g., when the ball is lost or out of bounds.

20-2. Dropping and Re-dropping

The dropping procedure is simple. The player has only to stand erect, hold the ball at shoulder height and arm's length—and drop it. He can face in any direction. There's no penalty for dropping in any other manner *provided* you take corrective action, which means re-dropping properly. Otherwise, it costs a stroke.

It's common for a ball dropped on a slope to roll more than two club-lengths or closer to the hole than its original position. Rule 20-2c spells out a three-step procedure:

1. Ball is dropped and it rolls nearer the hole than where it was at rest or more than two club-lengths after it is dropped.

2. Ball is dropped again. It does the same thing it did in Step 1.

3. Ball is then *placed* on the spot where it first touched a part of the course when it was dropped the second time.

The wording of Rule 20-2b was improved in 1992 to satisfy literalists who complained it was often impossible to comply with a direction to drop as near as possible to "the spot." The new language says the spot can be estimated when the specific spot is not known to the player.

20-3. Placing and Replacing

Placing naturally doesn't have the complications that go with dropping, but one aspect of the procedure needs study. What do you do when you have lifted the ball, are going to replace it, but your original lie is altered?

In a fairway, you then place your ball in "the nearest lie most similar to the orignal lie which is not more than one club-length from the original lie, not nearer the hole, and not in a hazard."

But in a bunker, the procedure is dramatically different. When a lie is altered—as often happens when balls come to rest adjacent to each other—the player whose lie was altered by the explosion shot of another player must *re-create* his original lie as nearly as possible. That might mean smoothing out the area with a rake, or it might mean having to push the ball into the sand. It depends on what the original lie was.

20-4. When Ball Dropped or Placed Is in Play

There's a classic Jack Nicklaus rules incident to serve as the illustration for teaching this clause.

Jack's ball came to rest against a stool to the right of the 15th green during a Masters Tournament. The ball moved when the stool was moved. Jack correctly replaced the ball which was then perched precariously on a bare spot. It was so tough a shot that the odds favored his getting down in three. But as Jack was looking over the situation, and before he addressed the ball, it moved—15 yards down the slope to the edge of the green. It was then in a position where a two-putt was a cinch.

Jack, thinking, "It can't be right that I get to play from this new position" conferred with an official stationed at that spot. The official told him to replace the ball. That's what's known as a bad ruling. The official was wrong.

Since the ball had been properly replaced and it had stayed at rest—for about a minute in this case—there was no requirement that it be replaced. In fact, it's a two-stroke penalty for doing so, even though the motive is good sportsmanship, as it was in Jack's case. But this incident teaches us another aspect of the Rules: There was no penalty because an official representing the Committee gave the ruling, and a player is entitled to assume that the ruling is correct.

20-6. Lifting Ball Wrongly Dropped or Placed

This clause gets the player off the hook if he errs in dropping or placing, provided he hasn't made the next stroke. Example: A player drops from a cart path—an obstruction—more than one club-length from the nearest point of relief. Another player reminds him the procedure is different than from a lateral water hazard. The player can then correct the mistake without penalty.

20-7. Playing from Wrong Place

Excuse me, but the language of this one is on the heavy side.

Go back to the illustration just offered in 20-6, where a player drops more than one club-length from the nearest point of relief from a cart path. But this time, imagine that the mistake is not corrected and the player plays on. That's what is meant by "playing from wrong place."

We also run into the words "serious breach" for the first time. That happens when playing from a wrong place gives a player an inordinate

Marking a Ball
When a ball anywhere on the course is to be lifted, its position must be marked if the ball is to be replaced. I use a coin (1) and place it immediately behind the ball (2) before lifting the ball (3). When the coin interferes with another player, it's moved the length of one or more putt-erheads. To make sure I can replace the ball exactly where it was, I first select a reference point—often a tree—before placing the toe of the putter next to the ball and placing the coin at the heel (4). (R. 20-1)

advantage in stroke play. The most common instance is when a player gets fouled up taking relief from a water hazard. Instead of dropping behind the hazard, the ball is dropped on the far side of the hazard—say 50 yards ahead of where it should have been dropped. That's a "serious breach" and if it's not corrected the penalty is disqualification.

RULE 21

CLEANING BALL

A ball on the putting green may be cleaned when lifted under Rule 16-1b. Elsewhere, a ball may be cleaned when lifted except when it has been lifted:

a. To determine if it is unfit for play (Rule 5-3);

b. For identification (Rule 12-2), in which case it may be cleaned only to the extent necessary for identification; or

c. Because it is interfering with or assisting play (Rule 22).

If a player cleans his ball during play of a hole except as provided in this Rule, *he shall incur a penalty of one stroke* and the ball, if lifted, shall be replaced.

If a player who is required to replace a ball fails to do so, *he shall incur the penalty* for breach of Rule 20-3a, but no additional penalty under Rule 21 shall be applied.

Exception: If a player incurs a penalty for failing to act in accordance with Rule 5-3, 12-2 or 22, no additional penalty under Rule 21 shall be applied.

In most cases, the ball may be cleaned when it's lifted. Rule 21 lists the three exceptions to that principle.

By the way, you can't clean your ball through the green just because something sticks to it—something that might affect the subsequent flight of the ball; e.g., mud or grass. You have to wait until the ball comes to rest on the putting green. Then it can be cleaned.

Ah, but there's a helpful decision about insects. It says a live insect on the ball is not considered to be adhering to the ball and is therefore not a loose impediment. So the player can gingerly remove the insect or blow it off (without lifting the ball).

RULE 22

BALL INTERFERING WITH OR ASSISTING PLAY

Any player may:

a. Lift his ball if he considers that the ball might assist any other player or

b. Have any other ball lifted if he considers that the ball might interfere with his play or assist the play of any other player,

but this may not be done while another ball is in motion. In stroke play, a player required to lift his ball may play first rather than lift. A ball lifted under this Rule shall be replaced.

If a ball is accidentally moved in complying with this Rule, no penalty is incurred and the ball shall be replaced.

PENALTY FOR BREACH OF RULE:
Match play — Loss of hole; Stroke play — Two strokes.
Note: *Except on the putting green, the ball may not be cleaned when lifted under this Rule — see Rule 21.*

Rule 22 covers all the situations in which a ball interferes with or assists play.

The tenets apply to both match and stroke play. Any player can have any ball lifted if he thinks it might interfere with his play or, because of its location, help the play of an opponent or fellow competitor.

I trust that most of us have long forgotten the pre-1984 Rule whereby the player away in match play was said to "control" the opponent's ball in the sense of having him leave or lift it. That's long gone.

In stroke play, when a competitor's ball is in position to help play of someone else, the competitor has an obligation to be fair to everyone else and lift his ball.

Example: A ball is six inches beyond the hole on the line of a player faced with a greenside bunker shot. The player whose ball is near the hole does nothing and the bunker shot is played. There's a Decision saying if this kind of thing goes on both players can be disqualified for agreeing to waive a Rule.

Another interesting Rule 22 Decision points out that a player can require another ball to be lifted on grounds of "mental interference" even if it's off the line of play. But don't try to pull that "mental interference" gambit to get relief from an obstruction. The interference has to be real in that instance.

RULE 23

LOOSE IMPEDIMENTS

Definition

"Loose impediments" are natural objects such as stones, leaves, twigs, branches and the like, dung, worms and insects and casts or heaps made by them, provided they are not fixed or growing, are not solidly embedded and do not adhere to the ball.

Sand and loose soil are loose impediments on the putting green but not elsewhere.

Snow and natural ice, other than frost, are either casual water or loose impediments, at the option of the player. Manufactured ice is an obstruction.

Dew and frost are not loose impediments.

23-1.
Relief

Except when both the loose impediment and the ball lie in or touch a hazard, any loose impediment may be removed without penalty. If the ball moves, see Rule 18-2c.

When a ball is in motion, a loose impediment which might influence the movement of the ball shall not be removed.

PENALTY FOR BREACH OF RULE:
Match play — Loss of hole; Stroke play — Two strokes.
(Searching for ball in hazard — see Rule 12-1.)
(Touching line of putt — see Rule 16-1a.)

A Bad Break
Because my ball lies in a hazard this twig may not be moved. The same applies to leaves, stones and other loose impediments—all natural objects. In a hazard you can't so much as touch one with your club on your backswing. Of course, if the twig were magically changed into a cigar, it could be removed because a cigar is an obstruction—an artificial object.
(R. 13-4)

Rule 23 is easy to understand and apply so long as you grasp the Definition which says loose impediments are natural objects not fixed or growing, not solidly embedded and not adhering to the ball.

There's one twist with regard to loose impediments: They can't be touched in a hazard. The common ramification of that structure means those leaves and stones interfering with your stroke can't be touched.

Here are some Decisions on loose impediments:

• If a stone is partially embedded (which I take to mean is not flat with the surface of the ground) and may be picked up with ease, it's a loose impediment. When in doubt, the stone should not be removed.

• The status of loose impediments can change. A log is one, but not after it's been converted into the seat of a bench.

• Ant hills are loose impediments. So are half-eaten pieces of fruit (even though they have been altered by man) and banana skins.

• Plugs of compacted soil thrown up by the maintainence process known as aerification are loose impediments even though other hunks of loose soil are not. Don't ask why. Just take this rare little gift from the rules-makers.

• It's OK to remove loose impediments from an area which you are about to drop in.

• A very fierce competitor named C. E. Miller once removed leaves beyond the hole as his opponent was getting ready to stroke a frightening downhill putt toward a lake. The opponent cried foul. He was right. Mr. Miller had no right to remove loose impediments which might have affected his opponent's play.

RULE 24

OBSTRUCTIONS

An "obstruction" is anything artificial, including the artificial surfaces and sides of roads and paths and manufactured ice, except:

a. Objects defining <u>out of bounds</u>, such as walls, fences, stakes and railings;

b. Any part of an immovable artificial object which is out of bounds; and

c. Any construction declared by the Committee to be an integral part of the course.

Definition

A player may obtain relief from a movable <u>obstruction</u> as follows:

a. If the ball does not lie in or on the obstruction, the obstruction may be removed. If the ball moves, it shall be replaced, and there is no penalty provided that the movement of the ball is directly attributable to the removal of the obstruction. Otherwise, Rule 18-2a applies.

b. If the ball lies in or on the obstruction, the ball may be lifted, without penalty, and the obstruction removed. The ball shall <u>through the green</u> or in a <u>hazard</u> be dropped, or on the <u>putting green</u> be placed, as near as possible to the spot directly under the place where the ball lay in or on the obstruction, but not nearer the hole.

The ball may be cleaned when lifted under Rule 24-1.

When a ball is in motion, an obstruction which might influence the movement of the ball, other than an attended flagstick or equipment of the players, shall not be removed.

24-1.
Movable Obstruction

a. INTERFERENCE

Interference by an immovable <u>obstruction</u> occurs when a ball lies in or on the obstruction, or so close to the obstruction that the obstruction interferes with the player's <u>stance</u> or the area of his intended swing. If the player's ball lies on the <u>putting green</u>, interference also occurs if an immovable obstruction on the <u>putting green</u> intervenes on his line of putt. Otherwise, intervention on the line of play is not, of itself, interference under this Rule.

b. RELIEF

Except when the ball lies in or touches a <u>water hazard</u> or a <u>lateral water hazard</u>, a player may obtain relief from interference by an immovable <u>obstruction</u>, without penalty, as follows:

(i) *Through the Green:* If the ball lies <u>through the green</u>, the point on the <u>course</u> nearest to where the ball lies shall be determined (without crossing over, through or under the obstruction) which (a) is not nearer the hole, (b) avoids interference (as defined) and (c) is not in a <u>hazard</u> or on a <u>putting green</u>. The player shall lift the ball and drop it within one club-length of the point thus determined on ground which fulfills (a), (b) and (c) above.

24-2.
Immovable Obstruction

Movable Obstruction
A rake is artificial and therefore an obstruction. Since it's easy to move, it's a movable obstruction. To obtain relief, I therefore prepare (1) to move it. Ah, but when I move the rake the ball moves too. I anticipated that and marked the original position of the ball with a tee (2). I am required to replace the ball (3). There is no penalty. (R. 24-1)

Note: *The prohibition against crossing over, through or under the* obstruction *does not apply to the artificial surfaces and sides of roads and paths or when the ball lies in or on the obstruction.*

(ii) *In a Bunker:* If the ball lies in or touches a bunker, the player shall lift and drop the ball in accordance with Clause (i) above, except that the ball must be dropped in the bunker.

(iii) *On the Putting Green:* If the ball lies on the putting green, the player shall lift the ball and place it in the nearest position to where it lay which affords relief from interference, but not nearer the hole nor in a hazard.

The ball may be cleaned when lifted under Rule 24-2b.

(Ball rolling to a position where there is interference by the condition from which relief was taken — see Rule 20-2c(v).)

Exception: A player may not obtain relief under Rule 24-2b if (a) it is clearly unreasonable for him to play a stroke because of interference by anything other than an immovable obstruction or (b) interference by an immovable obstruction would occur only through use of an unnecessarily abnormal stance, swing or direction of play.

Note: *If a ball lies in or touches a* water hazard *(including a* lateral water hazard*), the player is not entitled to relief without penalty from interference by an immovable obstruction. The player shall play the ball as it lies or proceed under Rule 26-1.*

c. BALL LOST

Except in a water hazard or a lateral water hazard, if there is

Immovable Obstruction

I'm entitled to relief without penalty because this irrigation control box interferes with my stance (1). The same applies in (2) because the box interferes with the area of my intended swing. But I get no relief in (3) because the obstruction, although on my line, does not interfere with my stance or swing. When you take relief from an immovable obstruction (4), you establish the nearest point, no nearer the hole, where there is no interference, and drop within one club-length of that point. (R. 24-2)

reasonable evidence that a ball is lost in an immovable obstruction, the player may, without penalty, substitute another ball and follow the procedure prescribed in Rule 24-2b. For the purpose of applying this Rule, the ball shall be deemed to lie at the spot where it entered the obstruction. If the ball is lost in an underground drain pipe or culvert the entrance to which is in a <u>hazard</u>, a ball must be dropped in that hazard or the player may proceed under Rule 26-1, if applicable.

PENALTY FOR BREACH OF RULE:
Match play — Loss of hole; Stroke play — Two strokes.

There's a tiny ray of added relief in the 1992 Rules when it comes to obstructions. A new clause provides that if there is "reasonable evidence"

that a ball is lost in an obstruction, it can be deemed to lie at the point where it entered the obstruction and dropped as per this rule. The ball is not treated as if it's lost.

In using Rule 24, don't over-read the word "relief." It doesn't mean you always get what you want. By no means does it guarantee you'll be able to play directly at the hole after dropping. There's no such thing as "line of sight" relief in the Rules. I'm afraid golfers are misled by what they see on television when "line of sight" relief is granted by Local Rule from "temporary immovable obstructions"—scoreboards, grandstands and the like—which are not a problem in everyday golf.

There are specific exclusions to the obstruction rule. There is no relief granted, even though the interfering object is artificial, when:

1. The object defines out of bounds—fences and even movable stakes.
2. Any part of an immovable object that is out of bounds.
3. Any construction declared by the Committee to be an "integral part of the course." A celebrated example is the road to the right of the 17th hole on the Old Course at St. Andrews, Scotland. The onus is on the Committee to identify any such limitation.
4. When the ball lies in a water hazard or lateral water hazard, the player is not entitled to relief from interference without penalty from an immovable obstruction, e.g., a pipe. Note that if the ball is outside the hazard but the obstruction is within the hazard, relief is permissible.

Relief from Cart Paths

An artificially surfaced cart path is an immovable obstruction. I'm entitled to relief because the ball lies on (1) the path, but I'd also get relief if the ball was off the path but I had to stand on it. After determining the nearest point of relief I measure (2) one club-length from that point and then drop in the permissible area (3). Note that nearest point of relief (4) is one place for a right-handed golfer, but it's another place (5) for a left-handed golfer. (R. 24-2)

Obstructions in Hazard
*The rake, cigarette, and cup are
all movable obstructions and
can be removed even though my
ball lies in a hazard. If the ball
moves, there is no penalty and
the ball must be replaced.*
(R. 24-1)

Some important guidelines in applying Rule 24:

• Whenever the artificial object is movable, it may be removed. Then the player does not have the option of treating it as immovable. It's either one or the other.

• Relief from movable obstructions is simple. Just move them. If the ball moves in the process, the ball must be replaced and there is no penalty.

• Be careful of sprinkler heads and the plastic caps of irrigation heads on the aprons of putting greens. Resist the impulse to lift and place the ball on side when one of these is on your line, especially when you want to putt the ball. There is relief only if the object interferes with your stance or swing. Ah, but—as sometimes happens with bad design—both the sprinkler head and ball are on the green, then you are entitled to relief.

Sprinkler Heads
Since this sprinkler head interferes with my stance (1) I'm entitled to relief without penalty. The same is true if the ball is on the sprinkler head (2). When I determine the nearest point of relief, I mark that point (3) with a tee. Then, I'm entitled to drop anywhere within one club-length (4) of that point no nearer the hole than the ball's original position. (R. 24-2)

RULE 25

ABNORMAL GROUND CONDITIONS AND WRONG PUTTING GREEN

Definitions   "Casual water" is any temporary accumulation of water on the <u>course</u> which is visible before or after the player takes his <u>stance</u> and is not in a <u>water hazard</u>.

Snow and natural ice, other than frost, are casual water or <u>loose impediments</u>, at the option of the player. Manufactured ice is an <u>obstruction</u>. Dew and frost are not casual water.

Immovable Obstruction in Hazard

Here we have a ball on a bridge over troubled water. Because the bridge is within a water hazard, you may not drop the ball without penalty (R. 24-2), but you are allowed to ground your club on the bridge (R. 13-4). You may also, under penalty of one stroke, proceed under the water hazard Rule. (R. 26-1)

"Ground under repair" is any portion of the <u>course</u> so marked by order of the Committee or so declared by its authorized representative. It includes material piled for removal and a hole made by a greenkeeper, even if not so marked. Stakes and lines defining ground under repair are in such ground. The margin of ground under repair extends vertically downwards, but not upwards.

Note 1: *Grass cuttings and other material left on the course which have been abandoned and are not intended to be removed are not ground under repair unless so marked.*

Note 2: *The Committee may make a Local Rule prohibiting play from ground under repair.*

25-1.

Casual Water, Ground Under Repair and Certain Damage to Course

a. INTERFERENCE

Interference by <u>casual water</u>, <u>ground under repair</u> or a hole, cast or runway made by a burrowing animal, a reptile or a bird occurs when a ball lies in or touches any of these conditions or

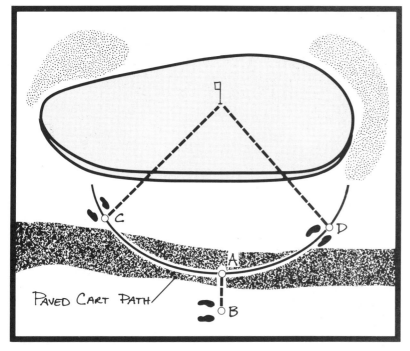

Dropping from an Obstruction

With the ball at (A) three spots might qualify as the nearest point of relief when there's interference by an immovable obstruction, such as a paved cart path. The point that is the shortest distance from the ball (A) must be used.

The three possibilities are behind the obstruction (B); on an arc to the left (C); and on an arc to the right (D). Since line A-B is shorter than lines A-C and A-D, the nearest point of relief is B. The same principle applies when relief is taken from ground under repair and casual water. (R. 24-2b)

when such a condition on the <u>course</u> interferes with the player's <u>stance</u> or the area of his intended swing.

If the player's ball lies on the <u>putting green</u>, interference also occurs if such condition on the putting green intervenes on his line of putt.

If interference exists, the player may either play the ball as it lies (unless prohibited by Local Rule) or take relief as provided in Clause b.

b. RELIEF

If the player elects to take relief, he shall proceed as follows:

(i) *Through the Green:* If the ball lies <u>through the green</u>, the point on the <u>course</u> nearest to where the ball lies shall be determined which (a) is not nearer the hole, (b) avoids interference by the condition, and (c) is not in a <u>hazard</u> or on a <u>putting green</u>. The player shall lift the ball and drop it without penalty within one club-length of the point thus determined on ground which fulfills (a), (b) and (c) above.

(ii) *In a Hazard:* If the ball lies in or touches a <u>hazard</u>, the player shall lift and drop the ball either: .

(a) Without penalty, in the hazard, as near as possible to the spot where the ball lay, but not nearer the hole, on ground which affords maximum available relief from the condition;

or

(b) *Under penalty of one stroke,* outside the hazard, keeping the point where the ball lay directly between the hole and the spot on which the ball is dropped.

Exception: If a ball lies in or touches a <u>water hazard</u> (including

Casual Water

The ball lies in casual water (1) so I'm entitled to take relief by first determining the nearest point that avoids the casual water and is not nearer the hole. I haven't reached that point in (2) because my foot is in the water. That's interference. But in (3) I've determined the point and have marked it with a tee. I'm entitled to clean the ball (4) before dropping it within one club-length of the nearest point of relief (5). (R. 25-1)

Mandatory Relief
Here's an instance where you must take relief (but at least without penalty). If the Committee has, in a Local Rule, exercised its right to protect parts of the course—flower beds, turf nurseries—by requiring players to treat them as ground under repair, play is prohibited from such areas. (Def.—Ground Under Repair: Note 2)

a <u>lateral water hazard</u>), the player is not entitled to relief without penalty from a hole, cast or runway made by a burrowing animal, a reptile or a bird. The player shall play the ball as it lies or proceed under Rule 26-1.

(iii) *On the Putting Green:* If the ball lies on the <u>putting green</u>, the player shall lift the ball and place it without penalty in the nearest position to where it lay which affords maximum available relief from the condition, but not nearer the hole nor in a <u>hazard</u>.

The ball may be cleaned when lifted under Rule 25-1b.

(Ball rolling to a position where there is interference by the condition from which relief was taken — see Rule 20-2c(v).)

Exception: A player may not obtain relief under Rule 25-1b if (a) it is clearly unreasonable for him to play a stroke because of interference by anything other than a condition covered by Rule 25-1a or (b) interference by such a condition would occur only through use of an unnecessarily abnormal stance, swing or direction of play.

c. BALL LOST UNDER CONDITION COVERED BY RULE 25-1

It is a question of fact whether a ball lost after having been struck toward a condition covered by Rule 25-1 is lost under such condition. In order to treat the ball as lost under such condition, there must be reasonable evidence to that effect. In the absence of such evidence, the ball must be treated as a lost ball and Rule 27 applies.

(i) *Outside a Hazard* — If a ball is lost outside a hazard under a condition covered by Rule 25-1, the player may take relief as follows: the point on the course nearest to where the ball last crossed the margin of the area shall be determined which (a) is not nearer the hole than where the ball last crossed the margin, (b) avoids interference by the condition and (c) is not in a hazard or on a putting green. He shall drop a ball without penalty within one club-length of the point thus determined on ground which fulfills (a), (b) and (c) above.

(ii) *In a Hazard* — If a ball is lost in a hazard under a condition covered by Rule 25-1, the player may drop a ball either:

(a) Without penalty, in the hazard, as near as possible to the point at which the original ball last crossed the margin of the area, but not nearer the hole, on ground which affords maximum available relief from the condition;

or

(b) *Under penalty of one stroke,* outside the hazard, keeping the point at which the original ball last crossed the margin of the hazard directly between the hole and the spot on which the ball is dropped.

Exception: If a ball lies in a water hazard (including a lateral water hazard), the player is not entitled to relief without penalty for a ball lost in a hole, cast or runway made by a burrowing animal, a reptile or a bird. The player shall proceed under Rule 26-1.

25-2.
Embedded Ball

A ball embedded in its own pitch-mark in the ground in any closely mown area through the green may be lifted, cleaned and dropped, without penalty, as near as possible to the spot where it lay but not nearer the hole. "Closely mown area" means any area of the course, including paths through the rough, cut to fairway height or less.

25-3.
Wrong Putting Green

A player must not play a ball which lies on a putting green other than that of the hole being played. The ball must be lifted and the player must proceed as follows: The point on the course nearest to where the ball lies shall be determined which (a) is not nearer the hole and (b) is not in a hazard or on a putting green. The player shall lift the ball and drop it without penalty within one club-length of the point thus determined on ground which fulfills (a) and (b) above. The ball may be cleaned when so lifted.

Ground Under Repair

The relief procedure for ground under repair and casual water are the same. I can take relief if the ball is in ground under repair or if I have to stand in the area. Relief, of course, is optional. If I like the lie, I'll simply play the ball without taking relief. (R. 25-1)

Note: *Unless otherwise prescribed by the Committee, the term "a putting green other than that of the hole being played" includes a practice putting green or pitching green on the course.*
PENALTY FOR BREACH OF RULE:
Match play — Loss of hole; Stroke play — Two strokes.

25-1. Casual Water, Ground Under Repair and Certain Damage to the Course

The word "interference" is often misunderstood by readers of the Rules of Golf. They might do better to think "gets in the way of" or "intervenes" as definitions. Thus, you are entitled to relief not only because your ball lies in ground under repair or casual water but also if you have to stand in it, even though the ball lies outside the area. The same applies to burrowing animal holes (but not when the ball lies in or touches a water hazard). Determining "the point on the course nearest to where the ball lies" is the crux of applying Rule 25. It helps to think there are three possible points (see the diagram on p. 109) to consider every time, but only one of these is the nearest point in the sense that your ball will have traveled the shortest distance to reach that point. Once you find that point, you get an additional one club-length leeway.

The relief procedure on a putting green is markedly different. A determination is made to the nearest point that avoids the condition and the ball is then placed—not dropped—at that point.

By Definition, there is no such thing as casual water in a water hazard.

Here's how to treat some common ground-under-repair situations:
• A player has a bad lie in a large ground-under-repair area and would like to drop within the area in a good spot.

Answer: He can't do it. He must drop on ground that avoids the condition—*outside* the ground under repair.

• A player drops outside ground under repair as per Rule 25-1, but the ball rolls back into the ground-under-repair area. He likes the new lie. May he play? No. See Rule 20-2c.

• A player drops properly from ground under repair, but now his stance is in the area. Must he drop again? Yes.

• What can a golfer do when a bunker is completely covered with casual water?

Answer: He may drop in the bunker in the shallowest casual water as near as possible to the spot where the ball first lay, but not nearer the hole, or outside the bunker under penalty of one stroke.

• A player's ball is literally unplayable, in the crevice of a tree trunk. Making a stroke is impossible but when the player takes a stance he's in casual water. Is he entitled to relief under Rule 25?

Answer: No. See the Exception to Rule 25-1b which says no relief if the ball's position is such that an attempt to play a stroke would be "clearly unreasonable."

25-2. Embedded Ball

This is a situation you must be wary of. Relief is built into the Rules for balls embedded through the green in areas cut to fairway height or less. Essentially, that means no relief from balls embedded in the rough. But, and this is a very big but, Committees *may* extend the relief area to everything "through the green" which includes the rough.

This liberal extension is done every week on the PGA Tour and is done almost without exception by the USGA at its championships. But the average golfer, who tends to learn the Rules by what he sees on television, may not understand this subtle distinction and may very well get trapped by lifting a plugged ball from the rough at his home course.

In my view, the time is long past for the basic rule to cover all areas through the green.

25-3. Wrong Putting Green

You may not play from a wrong putting green, which includes a practice green. The relief procedure calls for a drop at a "nearest point" which invariably means a drop on an apron.

RULE 26

WATER HAZARDS (INCLUDING LATERAL WATER HAZARDS)

Definitions

A "water hazard" is any sea, lake, pond, river, ditch, surface drainage ditch or other open water course (whether or not containing water) and anything of a similar nature.

All ground or water within the margin of a water hazard is part of the water hazard. The margin of a water hazard extends vertically upwards and downwards. Stakes and lines defining the margins of water hazards are in the hazards.

Note: *Water hazards (other than <u>lateral water hazards</u>) should be defined by yellow stakes or lines.*

A "lateral water hazard" is a <u>water hazard</u> or that part of a water hazard so situated that it is not possible or is deemed by the Committee to be impracticable to drop a ball behind the water hazard in accordance with Rule 26-1b.

That part of a water hazard to be played as a lateral water hazard should be distinctively marked.

Note: *Lateral water hazards should be defined by red stakes or lines.*

26-1.
Ball in Water Hazard

It is a question of fact whether a ball lost after having been struck toward a <u>water hazard</u> is lost inside or outside the hazard. In order to treat the ball as lost in the hazard, there must be reasonable evidence that the ball lodged in it. In the absence of such evidence, the ball must be treated as a lost ball and Rule 27 applies.

If a ball lies in, touches or is lost in a water hazard (whether the ball lies in water or not), the player may *under penalty of one stroke:*

a. Play a ball as nearly as possible at the spot from which the original ball was last played (see Rule 20-5);

or

b. Drop a ball behind the water hazard, keeping the point at which the original ball last crossed the margin of the water hazard directly between the hole and the spot on which the ball is dropped, with no limit to how far behind the water hazard the ball may be dropped;

or

c. *As additional options available only if the ball lies in, touches or is lost in a lateral water hazard,* drop a ball outside the water hazard within two club-lengths of (i) the point where the original ball last crossed the margin of the water hazard or (ii) a point on the opposite margin of the water hazard equidistant from the hole. The ball must be dropped and come to rest not nearer the hole than the point where the original ball last crossed the margin of the water hazard.

The ball may be cleaned when lifted under this Rule.

(Ball moving in water in a water hazard — see Rule 14-6.)

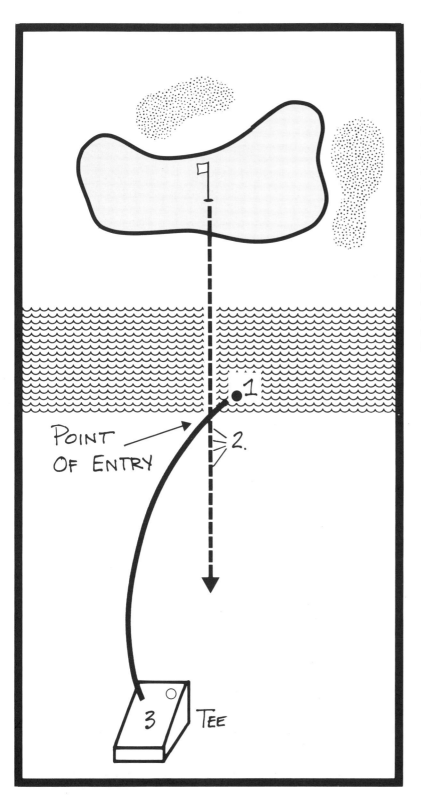

POINT OF ENTRY

Water Hazard Options
You can do one of three things when your ball comes to rest in a water hazard: (1) Assuming the ball is playable, go right ahead and play it without penalty. But if it's not playable, imagine a line (2) running from the hole to the point where the ball last crossed the margin of the hazard. You can drop any place on the course on an extension of that line for a penalty of one stroke.

The third option (3) is stroke-and-distance. In this illustration, that means returning to the tee, where your next stroke would be your third. Note that you can't drop along the line of the ball's flight. (R. 26-1)

Lateral Water Hazard Options

There are five options when a ball lies within a lateral water hazard. Three are the same as those for a water hazard: (1) Play the ball as it lies without penalty. (2) Drop behind the hazard on a line formed by the hole and point A where the ball entered the hazard with a one-stroke penalty added. (3) Use the stroke-and-distance option. The other two options also call for a penalty stroke. You may drop within two club-lengths of A, no nearer the hole (4) or on the opposite side of the hazard (5). The reference point on the opposite side is B, which is the same distance from the hole as A. (R. 26-1)

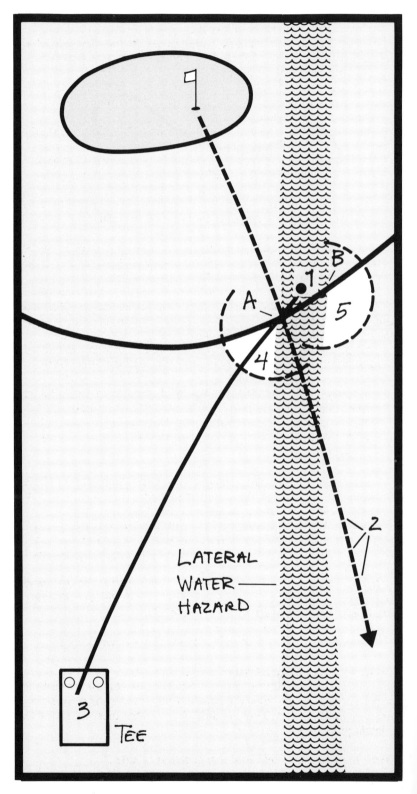

LATERAL WATER —— HAZARD

TEE

a. Ball Comes to Rest in Hazard

If a ball played from within a water hazard comes to rest in the hazard after the stroke, the player may:

(i) proceed under Rule 26-1; or

(ii) *under penalty of one stroke,* play a ball as nearly as possible at the spot from which the last stroke from outside the hazard was played (see Rule 20-5).

If the player proceeds under Rule 26-1a, he may elect not to play the dropped ball. If he so elects, he may:

a. Proceed under Rule 26-1b, *adding the additional penalty of one stroke* prescribed by that Rule;

or

b. Proceed under Rule 26-1c, if applicable, *adding the additional penalty of one stroke* prescribed by that Rule;

or

c. *Add an additional penalty of one stroke* and play a ball as nearly as possible at the spot from which the last stroke from outside the hazard was played (see Rule 20-5).

b. Ball Lost or Unplayable Outside Hazard or Out of Bounds

If a ball played from within a water hazard is lost or declared unplayable outside the hazard or is out of bounds, the player, after taking a *penalty of one stroke* under Rule 27-1 or 28a, may:

(i) play a ball as nearly as possible at the spot in the hazard from which the original ball was last played (see Rule 20-5);

or

(ii) proceed under Rule 26-1b, or if applicable Rule 26-1c, *adding the additional penalty of one stroke* prescribed by the Rule and using as the reference point the point where the original ball last crossed the margin of the hazard before it came to rest in the hazard;

or

(iii) *add an additional penalty of one stroke* and play a ball as nearly as possible at the spot from which the last stroke from outside the hazard was played (see Rule 20-5).

Note 1: *When proceeding under Rule 26-2b, the player is not required to drop a ball under Rule 27-1 or 28a. If he does drop a ball, he is not required to play it. He may alternatively proceed under Clause (ii) or (iii).*

Note 2: *If a ball played from within a water hazard is declared unplayable outside the hazard, nothing in Rule 26-2b precludes the player from proceeding under Rule 28b or c.*

Penalty for Breach of Rule:

Match play — Loss of hole; Stroke play — Two strokes.

26-2.
Ball Played Within Water Hazard

Water hazards and lateral water hazards should be marked by yellow or red (lateral) stakes and lines. There is bound to be confusion when they are not marked. Golfers should complain to the management when confronted with unmarked water hazards. It's not that hard to install and maintain proper markings.

Here are some hints toward the application of Rule 26:
• When you drop behind a water hazard, the ball itself must be dropped

on an imaginary line formed by the hole and the point where the ball last crossed the margin of the hazard. It doesn't matter where you stand; it's the position of the ball that matters.

● When dropping outside a water hazard or lateral water hazard, the options do not include dropping along what is sometimes called the "line of flight."

● You may not treat a ball as lost in a water hazard because it might be in the hazard. There must be "reasonable evidence" to that effect. Here's the language of the Decision on that point:

"The term 'reasonable evidence' in Rule 26-l is purposely and necessarily broad so as to permit sensible judgments to be reached on the basis of all the relevant circumstances of particular cases. As applied in this context, a player may not deem his ball lost in a water hazard simply because he thinks the ball may be in the hazard. The evidence must be preponderantly in favor of its being lost in the hazard. Otherwise, the ball must be considered lost outside the hazard and the player must proceed under Rule 27-1.

"Physical conditions in the area have a great deal to do with it. For example, if a water hazard is surrounded by a fairway on which a ball could hardly be lost, the existence of reasonable evidence that the ball is in the hazard would be more likely than there was deep rough in the area. Observing a ball splash in a water hazard would not necessarily provide reasonable evidence as splashing balls sometimes skip out of hazards. It would depend on all the circumstances."

RULE 27

BALL LOST OR OUT OF BOUNDS; PROVISIONAL BALL

If the original ball is lost in an immovable obstruction (Rule 24-2) or under a condition covered by Rule 25-1 (casual water, ground under repair and certain damage to the course), the player may proceed under the applicable Rule. If the original ball is lost in a water hazard, the player shall proceed under Rule 26.

Such Rules may not be used unless there is reasonable evidence that the ball is lost in an immovable obstruction, under a condition covered by Rule 25-1 or in a water hazard.

Definitions

A ball is "lost" if:

a. It is not found or identified as his by the player within five minutes after the player's side or his or their caddies have begun to search for it; or

b. The player has put another ball into play under the Rules, even though he may not have searched for the original ball; or

c. The player has played any stroke with a provisional ball from the place where the original ball is likely to be or from a point nearer the hole than that place, whereupon the provisional ball becomes the ball in play.

Time spent in playing a <u>wrong ball</u> is not counted in the five-minute period allowed for search.

"Out of bounds" is ground on which play is prohibited.

When out of bounds is defined by reference to stakes or a fence, or as being beyond stakes or a fence, the out of bounds line is determined by the nearest inside points of the stakes or fence posts at ground level excluding angled supports.

When out of bounds is defined by a line on the ground, the line itself is out of bounds.

The out of bounds line extends vertically upwards and downwards.

A ball is out of bounds when all of it lies out of bounds.

A player may stand out of bounds to play a ball lying within bounds.

A "provisional ball" is a ball played under Rule 27-2 for a ball which may be <u>lost</u> outside a <u>water hazard</u> or may be <u>out of bounds</u>.

If a ball is <u>lost</u> outside a <u>water hazard</u> or is <u>out of bounds</u>, the player shall play a ball, *under penalty of one stroke,* as nearly as possible at the spot from which the original ball was last played (see Rule 20-5).

Penalty for Breach of Rule 27-1:
Match play — Loss of hole; Stroke play — Two strokes.

27-1.
Ball Lost or Out of Bounds

a. Procedure

If a ball may be <u>lost</u> outside a <u>water hazard</u> or may be <u>out of bounds</u>, to save time the player may play another ball provisionally as nearly as possible at the spot from which the original ball was played (see Rule 20-5). The player shall inform his opponent in match play or his marker or a fellow-competitor in stroke play that he intends to play a <u>provisional ball</u>, and he shall play it before he or his partner goes forward to search for the original ball. If he fails to do so and plays another ball, such ball is not a provisional ball and becomes the <u>ball in play</u> *under penalty of stroke and distance* (Rule 27-1); the original ball is deemed to be lost.

b. When Provisional Ball Becomes Ball in Play

The player may play a provisional ball until he reaches the place where the original ball is likely to be. If he plays a stroke with the provisional ball from the place where the original ball is likely to be or from a point nearer the hole than that place, the original ball is deemed to be <u>lost</u> and the provisional ball becomes the ball in play, *under penalty of stroke and distance* (Rule 27-1).

If the original ball is lost outside a water hazard or is out of bounds, the provisional ball becomes the ball in play, *under penalty of stroke and distance* (Rule 27-1).

c. When Provisional Ball to Be Abandoned

If the original ball is neither lost outside a water hazard nor out of bounds, the player shall abandon the provisional ball and continue play with the original ball. If he fails to do so, any further strokes played with the provisional ball shall constitute playing a <u>wrong ball</u>

27-2.
Provisional Ball

and the provisions of Rule 15 shall apply.

Note: *If the original ball lies in a water hazard, the player shall play the ball as it lies or proceed under Rule 26. If it is lost in a water hazard or unplayable, the player shall proceed under Rule 26 or 28, whichever is applicable.*

27.1 Ball Lost or Out of Bounds

Here we find what may well be golf's most disliked penalty—stroke and distance for a ball lost or out of bounds. If you play from the tee and your ball flies out of bounds or is lost (outside a water hazard), the next stroke is the third, not the second, and it must be played from the tee—not some point down the road.

Over the years, there have been experiments with softer penalty clauses for Rule 27. They all were found wanting. It appears that stroke and distance is here to stay.

Everyone agrees that the concept of allowing for the play of a provisional ball for a ball that may be lost or out of bounds is a good idea. It saves time and trouble. If the penalty was distance only (so that the next stroke from the tee counted as the second stroke), we would see the provisional ball used not only as a time-saver but as a "Mulligan"—a way of getting off the hook for playing a bad shot.

Try this scenario: It's a par-3 hole with a veritable jungle off the right of the green. My ball flies into the jungle and the odds are it is either lost or unplayable. I'm looking at a 5. If Rule 27 called for distance only, my provisional ball would count as my second stroke. This time I knock it stiff! I'd be entitled to forget my original ball. I'm not required to search for it. I'd tap in for a 3—which I don't feel I deserve. In brief, it would be ludicrous to allow situations to develop in which it would sometimes be in the player's interest to lose a ball.

Some argue that the stroke penalty is acceptable, but why the torture of distance, too? If a ball goes out of bounds, why not allow players to drop within two club-lengths of the point where the ball crossed the margin of the boundary, à la the lateral water hazard condition? Because common sense demands that the procedures be the same for balls lost or out of bounds. Wild shots are often hit in the direction of boundaries but the ball isn't found. It might be out of bounds; it might just as well be lost in the woods on the course. Since there's no way of knowing for sure where the ball is, the only fair resolution is a Rule in which the two possibilities are given like treatment.

Here is what some Decisions have to say about lost balls:

• When a search goes beyond five minutes, the ball is plain lost. If a player subsequently finds the original and plays it, he plays a wrong ball. See Rule 15 for a summary of all the bad things that befall a player who plays a wrong ball.

• A player plays a sensational shot with a provisional ball, then goes into the woods and finds his original ball. We're dealing here with a question of fact. The player refuses to identify the found ball as his and proceeds to play his provisional. Is that fair? No, it sure isn't. Not only did play of the provisional in this case constitute playing a wrong ball, but the Committee would be justified in disqualifying a player who dishonestly refuses to identify his ball.

• A player searches for two minutes, declares his ball is lost and heads back to the tee. The ball is then found. The original ball remains the ball in play. There is no such animal as a "declaration" of a lost ball.

• Imagine the same situation as above, but this time the original shot was played from a fairway. Again, the player searches for only two minutes, declares the original is lost, walks back and drops another ball. The original is found within five minutes of the start of the search. This time the original is lost because the dropped ball became the ball in play—Rule 20-4.

27-2. Provisional Ball

The provisional ball is a welcome time-saver. It is often violated by golfers who mistakenly think they can play one when the original ball might be in any kind of difficulty. Here are some pitfalls:

• Beware of water hazards in the context of provisional balls. Say a ball is hit toward a water hazard flanked by trees and rough. A provisional ball may be played since the ball might be lost outside the hazard. But if the original is found within the water hazard the provisional must be abandoned. Play carries on as if the provisional was never played.

• The Rule does not permit a provisional ball for a ball that might be in a water hazard. But if a confused player announces he's playing a provisional ball *only* because his original might have found a water hazard, that ball automatically becomes the ball in play and the golfer now lies 3.

• After a provisional ball is played, the original is discovered unplayable. The provisional ball must be abandoned. Play continues under Rule 28, which governs unplayable balls.

• Rule 27-2 insists that the play of a provisional ball be preceded by an announcement. A grunt of dissatisfaction or an oath does not satisfy the requirement. Absent an announcement, the second ball automatically becomes the ball in play and the player then lies 3, even though the original ball is found in bounds.

RULE 28

BALL UNPLAYABLE

The player may declare his ball unplayable at any place on the course except when the ball lies in or touches a water hazard. The player is the sole judge as to whether his ball is unplayable.

If the player deems his ball to be unplayable, he shall, *under penalty of one stroke:*

a. Play a ball as nearly as possible at the spot from which the original ball was last played (see Rule 20-5);

or

b. Drop a ball within two club-lengths of the spot where the ball lay, but not nearer the hole;

or

c. Drop a ball behind the point where the ball lay, keeping that point directly between the hole and the spot on which the ball is dropped, with no limit to how far behind that point the ball may be dropped.

Unplayable Lie Options
You have three choices when you declare a ball unplayable through the green: (1) Go back and play from the spot where the previous stroke was played. (2) Drop a ball within two club-lengths of the spot where the ball was declared unplayable, no nearer the hole, as shown by the white area. Or (3) imagine a line from the hole to the ball and drop back on an extension of that line. In each instance there is a penalty of one stroke. If the ball is unplayable in a bunker, the stroke-and-distance option (1) is still available. Options 2 and 3, however, are modified to the extent that the ball must be dropped within the bunker if either option is used. Remember that a ball can't be declared unplayable in a water hazard. (R. 28)

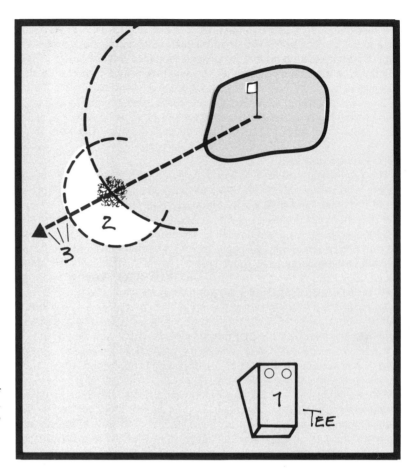

If the unplayable ball lies in a <u>bunker</u>, the player may proceed under Clause a, b or c. If he elects to proceed under Clause b or c, a ball must be dropped in the bunker.

The ball may be cleaned when lifted under this Rule.

PENALTY FOR BREACH OF RULE:
Match play — Loss of hole; Stroke play — Two strokes.

The USGA says it receives more grief on one fine point of Rule 28 than anything else in the Rules. There was a common failure to understand that when a ball in a bunker was declared unplayable the player could always fall back on the stroke and distance penalty as one of the options. In fact, you can *always* use the stroke and distance penalty.

The 1992 Rules changes include an amendment in the wording to underscore the availability of the stroke and distance option.

Rule 28 decisions include:

• When a ball is unplayable in a tree, and you want to exercise that option which allows dropping within two club-lengths, determine the spot directly beneath the ball in the tree and then use Rule 28 just as if the ball was unplayable on the ground.

● Be careful! If you drop from one unplayable lie into another, you don't get a second free chance. The dropped ball is also unplayable. The same applies when you drop off a cart path and the ball dropped is unplayable. Moral: Know what you are doing before you pick up a ball and drop it.

OTHER FORMS OF PLAY

THREESOMES AND FOURSOMES

Definitions

Threesome: A match in which one plays against two, and each side plays one ball.

Foursome: A match in which two play against two, and each side plays one ball.

29-1.
General

In a threesome or a foursome, during any <u>stipulated round</u> the partners shall play alternately from the teeing grounds and alternately during the play of each hole. <u>Penalty strokes</u> do not affect the order of play.

29-2.
Match Play

If a player plays when his partner should have played, *his side shall lose the hole.*

29-3.
Stroke Play

If the partners play a stroke or strokes in incorrect order, such stroke or strokes shall be cancelled and *the side shall incur a penalty of two strokes.* The side shall correct the error by playing a ball in correct order as nearly as possible at the spot from which it first played in incorrect order (see Rule 20-5). If the side plays a stroke from the next <u>teeing ground</u> without first correcting the error or, in the case of the last hole of the round, leaves the <u>putting green</u> without declaring its intention to correct the error, *the side shall be disqualified.*

Rule 29 is almost never referred to in the United States, because a threesome is virtually an extinct form of play and we seldom play foursomes which is a pity, because foursomes are a lot of fun.

Focus on the Definition. A threesome is not three people playing together. It's an odd form of play in which one side plays against two, and the two play alternate strokes with one ball.

A foursome is not four golfers playing together. It's that form of competition you see in the Ryder Cup or Walker Cup matches when two play against two with each team using only one ball, playing alternate strokes. It's often, and incorrectly, labeled "Scotch" foursomes.

Now that I think of it, there's so much confusion on this point that we need a new word or phrase to describe four players playing recreational golf together—something other than "foursome." Suggestions will be gratefully accepted.

RULE 30

THREE-BALL, BEST-BALL AND FOUR-BALL MATCH PLAY

Definitions

Three-Ball: A match play competition in which three play against one another, each playing his own ball. Each player is playing two distinct matches.

Best-Ball: A match in which one plays against the better ball of two or the best ball of three players.

Four-Ball: A match in which two play their better ball against the better ball of two other players.

30-1.
Rules of Golf Apply

The Rules of Golf, so far as they are not at variance with the following special Rules, shall apply to three-ball, best-ball and four-ball matches.

30-2.
Three-Ball Match Play

a. BALL AT REST MOVED BY AN OPPONENT

Except as otherwise provided in the Rules, if the player's ball is touched or moved by an opponent, his caddie or equipment other than during search, Rule 18-3b applies. *That opponent shall incur a penalty stroke in his match with the player,* but not in his match with the other opponent.

b. BALL DEFLECTED OR STOPPED BY AN OPPONENT ACCIDENTALLY

If a player's ball is accidentally deflected or stopped by an opponent, his caddie or equipment, no penalty shall be incurred. In his match with that opponent the player may play the ball as it lies or, before another stroke is played by either side, he may cancel the stroke and play a ball without penalty as nearly as possible at the spot from which the original ball was last played (see Rule 20-5). In his match with the other opponent, the ball shall be played as it lies.

Exception: Ball striking person attending flagstick — see Rule 17-3b.

(Ball purposely deflected or stopped by opponent — see Rule 1-2.)

30-3.
Best-Ball and Four-Ball Match Play

a. REPRESENTATION OF SIDE

A side may be represented by one partner for all or any part of a match; all partners need not be present. An absent partner may join a match between holes, but not during play of a hole.

b. MAXIMUM OF FOURTEEN CLUBS

The side shall be penalized for a breach of Rule 4-4 by any partner.

c. ORDER OF PLAY

Balls belonging to the same side may be played in the order the side considers best.

d. WRONG BALL

If a player plays a stroke with a wrong ball except in a hazard, *he shall be disqualified for that hole,* but his partner incurs no penalty even if the wrong ball belongs to him. If the wrong ball belongs to another player, its owner shall place a ball on the spot from which the wrong ball was first played.

e. DISQUALIFICATION OF SIDE

(i) *A side shall be disqualified* for a breach of any of the following by any partner:

Rule 1-3 — Agreement to Waive Rules.
Rule 4-1, -2 or -3 — Clubs.
Rule 5-1 or -2 — The Ball.
Rule 6-2a — Handicap (playing off higher handicap).
Rule 6-4 — Caddie.
Rule 6-7 — Undue Delay (repeated offense).
Rule 14-3 — Artificial Devices and Unusual Equipment.

(ii) *A side shall be disqualified* for a breach of any of the following by all partners:

Rule 6-3 — Time of Starting and Groups.
Rule 6-8 — Discontinuance of Play.

f. EFFECT OF OTHER PENALTIES

If a player's breach of a Rule assists his partner's play or adversely affects an opponent's play, *the partner incurs the applicable penalty in addition to any penalty incurred by the player.*

In all other cases where a player incurs a penalty for breach of a Rule, the penalty shall not apply to his partner. Where the penalty is stated to be loss of hole, the effect shall be to disqualify the player for that hole.

g. ANOTHER FORM OF MATCH PLAYED CONCURRENTLY

In a best-ball or four-ball match when another form of match is played concurrently, the above special Rules shall apply.

Beyond question, the most popular form of play is four-ball match play, which means two playing their better ball on each hole against the better ball of two others. It's almost always done on a handicap basis. The USGA Handicap System calls for the player with the lowest handicap to play off scratch (no handicaps strokes for her) and the others to key off her handicap, i.e., if she's a 10, a 12 gets two strokes in this match.

Rule 30 also covers Best-Ball (when one player goes up against the best ball of either two or three others) and Three-Ball (when three play against one another, each playing his own ball). But these two forms of play have become rare. Let's concentrate then on common four-ball match play.

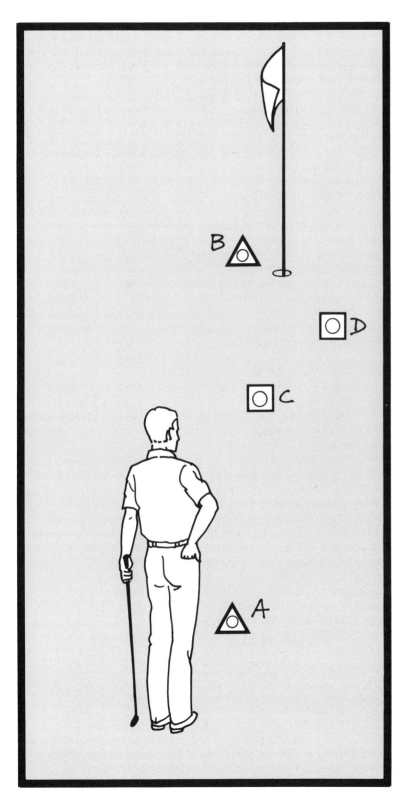

Four-Ball Match Play

In a four-ball match, any player can have any ball lifted before a stroke is made. In this illustration, A and B are partners and it is A's turn to putt. He will surely require that C's ball be lifted, since it's on his line. A would probably like B's ball to stay right where it is, since it could serve as a useful backstop, but either C or D can require B to lift his ball. As for ball D, it's off the line of putt, but A can have it lifted if it bothers him.

If any ball is not lifted and is struck by ball A, there is no penalty. A would play from where his ball then lies, while the owner of the displaced ball, whether he's A's partner or opponent, must replace it. (R. 30)

Most problems occur on the greens. As usual, we'll deal with A and B versus C and D.

CASE 1: A is away and B's ball is inches beyond the hole in such a position that it might well assist Ms. A in the play of her ball—as a backstop. True, but either C or D (as we learned back in Rule 22) can require that B's ball be lifted.

CASE 2: Now B's ball is on A's line. Naturally, A and B want the ball lifted. They may do so.

CASE 3: Now picture C's ball just past the hole, where it might be of help to A. C can lift her ball.

CASE 4: C's ball is on A's line. A can require C to lift her ball. Note: C does not have the option of putting out.

But now let's assume that in every case no ball is marked and lifted. A putts and strikes any other ball. Easy and consistent answer. There's no penalty; A plays from where she then lies; and the owner of the moved ball—be she friend or foe—must replace her ball.

In everyday golf, there is all kinds of action going on. Singles matches are played concurrent with the four-ball match. This imposes a strain on the Rules, but it's doable. According to Rule 30-3g, the four-ball Rules have priority. Example: If a partner concedes an opponent's putt, that does it—even though the other partner, who is involved in a separate singles match, wishes the putt wasn't conceded.

Other important elements in four-ball play:
• There is the strategic option which allows B to play, even though partner A is away.
• If your ball is deflected by your partner, caddie or equipment (including a cart you are sharing), you are disqualified for that hole, but your partner is not.
• When your ball is deflected by something on the opponent's side, there is no penalty, but you get a choice. Play the ball as it lies or replay the stroke.
• When a player violates a Rule, her partner is not penalized unless the nature of the violation helps her partner or hurts the play of an opponent.
• If one player on a team is late, or never shows up at all, the remaining player can play against the other team. The missing player can join the match in progress at the start of any hole.

RULE 31

FOUR-BALL STROKE PLAY

In four-ball stroke play two competitors play as partners, each playing his own ball. The lower score of the partners is the score for the hole. If one partner fails to complete the play of a hole, there is no penalty.

31-1.
Rules of Golf Apply

The Rules of Golf, so far as they are not at variance with the following special Rules, shall apply to four-ball stroke play.

A side may be represented by either partner for all or any part of a <u>stipulated round</u>; both partners need not be present. An absent competitor may join his partner between holes, but not during play of a hole.

The side shall be penalized for a breach of Rule 4-4 by either partner.

The marker is required to record for each hole only the gross score of whichever partner's score is to count. The gross scores to count must be individually identifiable; otherwise *the side shall be disqualified.* Only one of the partners need be responsible for complying with Rule 6-6b.
(Wrong score — see Rule 31-7a.)

Balls belonging to the same side may be played in the order the side considers best.

If a competitor plays a stroke with a <u>wrong ball</u> except in a <u>hazard</u>, he shall add *two penalty strokes to his score for the hole* and shall then play the correct ball. His partner incurs no penalty even if the wrong ball belongs to him.
If the wrong ball belongs to another competitor, its owner shall place a ball on the spot from which the wrong ball was first played.

a. BREACH BY ONE PARTNER
A side shall be disqualified from the competition for a breach of any of the following by either partner:
Rule 1-3 — Agreement to Waive Rules.
Rule 3-4 — Refusal to Comply with Rule.
Rule 4-1, -2 or -3 — Clubs.
Rule 5-1 or -2 — The Ball.
Rule 6-2b — Handicap (playing off higher handicap; failure to record handicap).
Rule 6-4 — Caddie.
Rule 6-6b — Signing and Returning Card.
Rule 6-6d — Wrong Score for Hole, i.e., when the recorded score of the partner whose score is to count is lower than actually taken. If the recorded score of the partner whose score is to count is higher than actually taken, it must stand as returned.
Rule 6-7 — Undue Delay (repeated offense).
Rule 7-1 — Practice Before or Between Rounds.
Rule 14-3 — Artificial Devices and Unusual Equipment.
Rule 31-4 — Gross Scores to Count Not Individually Identifiable.
b. BREACH BY BOTH PARTNERS
A side shall be disqualified:
(i) for a breach by both partners of Rule 6-3 (Time of Starting and Groups) or Rule 6-8 (Discontinuance of Play), or
(ii) if, at the same hole, each partner is in breach of a Rule the

penalty for which is disqualification from the competition or for a hole.

c. FOR THE HOLE ONLY

In all other cases where a breach of a Rule would entail disqualification, *the competitor shall be disqualified only for the hole at which the breach occurred.*

31-8.
Effect of Other Penalties

If a competitor's breach of a Rule assists his partner's play, *the partner incurs the applicable penalty in addition to any penalty incurred by the competitor.*

In all other cases where a competitor incurs a penalty for breach of a Rule, the penalty shall not apply to his partner.

Four-ball stroke play Rules differ from four-ball match play Rules when it comes to a ball moved by another ball. In four-ball stroke play, when a ball is putted from a putting green and strikes another ball on the green, the player who putted is penalized two strokes. The moved ball must be replaced. (In four-ball match play there is no penalty.)

Partners in four-ball stroke play may not "use" each other's balls as backstops. As in individual stroke play, the overriding principle is that the entire field has rights and must be protected against collusion. So if A is about to play from a bunker and the ball of partner B is just past the hole, B's ball must be removed. A and B should handle this detail by themselves. If they are remiss, it's up to C and D to protect the rest of the field by requiring that B's ball be lifted.

Rule 31 is usually adopted to serve another purpose—to control best-ball-of-four competitions—those in which each four-man team counts only the best score on a hole. Another standard variation is the pro-amateur format, which has the pro record his own score for every hole (because he's engaged in a stroke play competition against all the other pros) while at the same time helping his amateur partners in a best-ball-of-four competition.

RULE 32

BOGEY, PAR AND STABLEFORD COMPETITIONS

32-1.
Conditions

Bogey, par and Stableford competitions are forms of stroke competition in which play is against a fixed score at each hole. The Rules for stroke play, so far as they are not at variance with the following special Rules, apply.

a. BOGEY AND PAR COMPETITIONS

The reckoning for bogey and par competitions is made as in match play. Any hole for which a competitor makes no return shall be regarded as a loss. The winner is the competitor who is most successful in the aggregate of holes.

The marker is responsible for marking only the gross number of strokes for each hole where the competitor makes a net score equal to or less than the fixed score.

Note: *Maximum of 14 clubs — Penalties as in match play — see Rule 4-4.*

b. STABLEFORD COMPETITIONS

The reckoning in Stableford competitions is made by points awarded in relation to a fixed score at each hole as follows:

Hole Played In	Points
More than one over fixed score or no score returned	0
One over fixed score	1
Fixed score	2
One under fixed score	3
Two under fixed score	4
Three under fixed score	5
Four under fixed score	6

The winner is the competitor who scores the highest number of points.

The marker shall be responsible for marking only the gross number of strokes at each hole where the competitor's net score earns one or more points.

Note: *Maximum of 14 clubs (Rule 4-4) — Penalties applied as follows: From total points scored for the round, deduction of two points for each hole at which any breach occurred; maximum deduction per round: four points.*

32-2.
Disqualification Penalties

a. FROM THE COMPETITION

A competitor shall be disqualified from the competition for a breach of any of the following:

Rule 1-3 — Agreement to Waive Rules.
Rule 3-4 — Refusal to Comply with Rule.
Rule 4-1, -2 or -3 — Clubs.
Rule 5-1 or -2 — The Ball.
Rule 6-2b — Handicap (playing off higher handicap; failure to record handicap).
Rule 6-3 — Time of Starting and Groups.
Rule 6-4 — Caddie.
Rule 6-6b — Signing and Returning Card.
Rule 6-6d — Wrong Score for Hole, except that no penalty shall be incurred when a breach of this Rule does not affect the result of the hole.
Rule 6-7 — Undue Delay (repeated offense).
Rule 6-8 — Discontinuance of Play.
Rule 7-1 — Practice Before or Between Rounds.
Rule 14-3 — Artificial Devices and Unusual Equipment.

b. FOR A HOLE

In all other cases where a breach of a Rule would entail disqualification, *the competitor shall be disqualified only for the hole at which the breach occurred.*

Stableford competitions were about as common as free lunches in this country until a version of Stableford scoring was used as the basis for deciding a PGA Tour event—The International played outside Denver.

While The International is an individual competition, the Stableford is more often applied to team events. They're a lot of fun at the club level because they allow players of every skill level to suffer and exult together.

A common Stableford sends out teams of four, each using full handicap. A net score of double bogey, or worse, earns no points for a player on a hole, but a net bogey is worth 1 point, a par 2 points, and so on right up to 6 points for a score of 1 on a par-5 hole. (I've played my share of golf with creative high-handicap golfers, but never have I seen a net score of 1 on a par-5 hole.)

"Stableford" is a man's name, in fact, the only surname incorporated into the Rules of Golf. He was Dr. Frank B. Stableford of Great Britain, a surgeon and first-rate golfer, who invented the scoring system that bears his name. We know for a fact that the very first Stableford tournament was played on May 16, 1932, on the Wallsey Links, Cheshire, England.

ADMINISTRATION

THE COMMITTEE

The Committee shall lay down the conditions under which a competition is to be played.

The Committee has no power to waive a Rule of Golf.

Certain special rules governing stroke play are so substantially different from those governing match play that combining the two forms of play is not practicable and is not permitted. The results of matches played and the scores returned in these circumstances shall not be accepted.

In stroke play the Committee may limit a referee's duties.

33-1.
Conditions; Waiving Rule

a. DEFINING BOUNDS AND MARGINS

The Committee shall define accurately:
   (i) the <u>course</u> and <u>out of bounds</u>,
   (ii) the margins of <u>water hazards</u> and <u>lateral water hazards</u>,
   (iii) <u>ground under repair</u>, and
   (iv) <u>obstructions</u> and integral parts of the course.

b. NEW HOLES

New holes should be made on the day on which a stroke competition begins and at such other times as the Committee considers necessary, provided all competitors in a single round play with each hole cut in the same position.

Exception: When it is impossible for a damaged hole to be repaired so that it conforms with the Definition, the Committee may make a new hole in a nearby similar position.

c. PRACTICE GROUND

Where there is no practice ground available outside the area of a competition <u>course</u>, the Committee should lay down the area on

33-2.
The Course

which players may practice on any day of a competition, if it is practicable to do so. On any day of a stroke competition, the Committee should not normally permit practice on or to a <u>putting green</u> or from a <u>hazard</u> of the competition course.

d. COURSE UNPLAYABLE

If the Committee or its authorized representative considers that for any reason the course is not in a playable condition or that there are circumstances which render the proper playing of the game impossible, it may, in match play or stroke play, order a temporary suspension of play or, in stroke play, declare play null and void and cancel all scores for the round in question. When play has been temporarily suspended, it shall be resumed from where it was discontinued, even though resumption occurs on a subsequent day. When a round is cancelled, all penalties incurred in that round are cancelled.

(Procedure in discontinuing play — see Rule 6-8.)

33-3.
Times of Starting and Groups

The Committee shall lay down the times of starting and, in stroke play, arrange the groups in which competitors shall play.

When a match play competition is played over an extended period, the Committee shall lay down the limit of time within which each round shall be completed. When players are allowed to arrange the date of their match within these limits, the Committee should announce that the match must be played at a stated time on the last day of the period unless the players agree to a prior date.

33-4.
Handicap Stroke Table

The Committee shall publish a table indicating the order of holes at which handicap strokes are to be given or received.

33-5.
Score Card

In stroke play, the Committee shall issue for each competitor a score card containing the date and the competitor's name or, in foursome or four-ball stroke play, the competitors' names.

In stroke play, the Committee is responsible for the addition of scores and application of the handicap recorded on the card.

In four-ball stroke play, the Committee is responsible for recording the better-ball score for each hole and in the process applying the handicaps recorded on the card, and adding the better-ball scores.

In bogey, par and Stableford competitions, the Committee is responsible for applying the handicap recorded on the card and determining the result of each hole and the overall result or points total.

33-6.
Decision of Ties

The Committee shall announce the manner, day and time for the decision of a halved match or of a tie, whether played on level terms or under handicap.

A halved match shall not be decided by stroke play. A tie in stroke play shall not be decided by a match.

33-7.
Disqualification Penalty; Committee Discretion

A penalty of disqualification may in exceptional individual cases be waived, modified or imposed if the Committee considers such action warranted.

Any penalty less than disqualification shall not be waived or modified.

a. POLICY

The Committee may make and publish Local Rules for abnormal conditions if they are consistent with the policy of the Governing Authority for the country concerned as set forth in Appendix I to these Rules.

b. WAIVING PENALTY

A penalty imposed by a Rule of Golf shall not be waived by a Local Rule.

33-8.
Local Rules

Rule 33 is a message to those in charge of a competition—the Committee—rather than to the player. But it behooves every golfer to know what Rule 33 is all about. Moreover, those who serve on Committees should know it inside out. Here's an analysis of each part of Rule 33.

33-1. Conditions: Waiving Rule

The conditions, e.g., whether it's stroke or match play and whether the Rules of Golf have been modified to allow for that dreadful condition known as "winter rules" to apply, should be spelled out in exquisite detail. They include the form of play, who is eligible to enter, the number of players in the field, the scheduling of rounds, and prizes.

Rule 33-1 says that stroke and match play are like oil and water. Golfers nevertheless go on attempting to combine the two forms of play. Inevitably, they encounter conflicts, such as the fundamental point as to when a ball not "away" is played. In match play, the opponent can recall that stroke; in stroke play, the stroke stands.

33-2. The Course

It's the responsibility of Committees to keep courses properly marked for everyday play—especially when it comes to the margins of water hazards, out of bounds and ground under repair.

When water hazards are not defined and players have to sort things out for themselves, they should bear in mind that the natural limit of a water hazard is the spot where the ground breaks down to form the depression containing the water. That's where lines and stakes defining the limits of water hazards should normally be placed.

The Committees' powers and limitations with respect to suspending play or cancelling a round are spelled out in Rule 33-2d.

In match play, all a Committee can do is suspend play and decide when play is to be resumed. Once a match starts and the course becomes unplayable, the results of the holes played before suspension of play are to stand as recorded. Any strokes taken on a hole not completed count. Play is resumed where the ball lay at the time of suspension. The match is never begun anew on the first tee.

In stroke play, the Committee can, at its discretion, either cancel an entire round or rule that play is to be resumed where it was discontinued—even on a later day. On the PGA Tour, our Committee seldom cancels a round once play has started because the Tour has a powerful interest in finishing things up on Sunday; many of us have other commitments for Monday and television wants us to finish on Sunday.

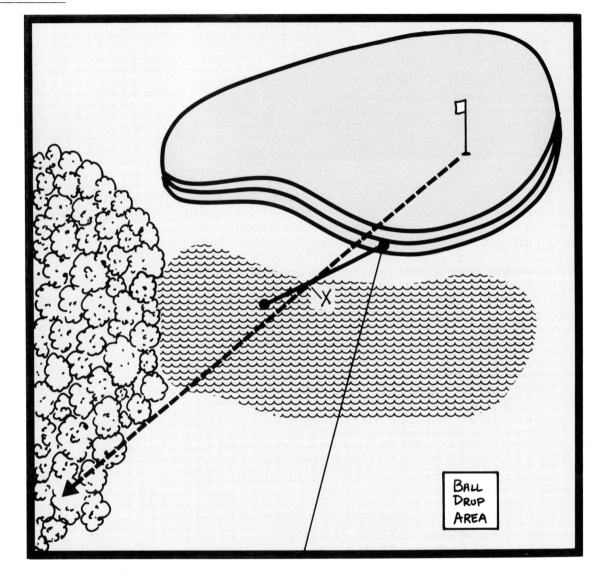

Ball-Drop Areas

Committees can install special ball-drop areas when it's impractical or unfair to limit players to the standard water hazard options.

Take this hole, which has a pond directly in front of the green and a slope between the pond and the elevated green. Balls often carry beyond the hazard into the slope but then carom back into the hazard. Often dropping behind the point where the ball last *entered the hazard (X) on an extension of a line between the point and the hole means the player would have to drop into a veritable jungle.*

The stroke-and-distance option, of course, is always available, but that seems too severe. So the Committee installs a clearly defined ball-drop area (lower right), which the player may use for the customary penalty of one stroke.

The main point is that Committees are all-powerful in this regard and have different priorities. What's best for the Tour may not be best for a club member-guest tournament.

33-3. Times of Starting and Groups

Club match play events are often fouled up by a failure of Committees to specify and enforce time limits for the play of rounds. The inability or unwillingness of opponents to get together for a match can spoil a tournament. One way to forestall such a delay is to assign starting times in advance to every match in every round but to allow any match to be played at another time, or even on another day, provided the match is completed prior to the time and date established for the next round.

33-4. Handicap Stroke Table

The order in which handicap strokes are allocated appears on all club scoreboards. The USGA Handicap System contains a section suggesting to clubs the method for assigning priorities. Meanwhile, USGA statisticians have figured out it makes little or no difference over the long run on which holes the strokes are taken. That is to say, it doesn't matter whether a handicap stroke is taken on a par-3 hole or a par-5 hole because it all seems to even out. What does matter is that the total number of strokes between opponents be equitable.

33-5. Score Card

Score cards are required only in stroke play. In match play they are a convenience, but all that matters is that the opponents agree on the status and conclusion of the match. They are not required to sign or return a card.

The Committee bears the responsibility for addition. The player must enter the correct number for each hole but if the player chooses to do the addition and makes an error, it's not his problem. The Committee has to do the addition separately and get it right.

33-6. Decision of Ties

Committees often fail to announce in advance what they plan to do in the event of a tie. Whenever they fail to do so, someone is unhappy because the method selected after the fact is bound to affect the humor of the player who loses out.

33-7. Disqualification Penalty; Committee Discretion

Let's take a couple of examples of what this section means:

• Rule 6-3 says that a player is to be disqualified if she arrives late at the first tee. But suppose the player was about to turn into the club driveway in plenty of time when she spots a fire in a house. She stops, runs into the house, saves a child and calls the fire department. Then she completes her journey to the course. The Committee should certainly waive any penalty.

Note that the Committee can modify or waive a disqualification penalty, but that it exceeds its powers if it waives or modifies any penalties less than disqualification.

There is a Decision that says a Committee is not justified in modifying the DQ penalty that results when a player returns an incorrect score because he did not know he had violated a rule.

Take the Paul Azinger case in the Doral tournament in 1991. Paul inadvertently violated a rule when he moved stones in a water hazard in the process of taking his stance. That is a two-stroke penalty, but Paul was disqualified for returning a wrong score. The Committee—in that instance the PGA Tour field staff—was vilified by media for not modifying the penalty. The point is: the Committee, no matter what its personal views, had no choice. The Decision carries the weight of golfing law. Either you play by the Rules, which include its Decisions, or you don't.

33-8. Local Rules

As a condition of play, a Committee says it's OK to tamp down something it calls "spike marks." In doing so, it has waived Rule 16-1. The game is now being played under something other than the Rules of Golf. It's time to get a new Committee.

RULE 34

DISPUTES AND DECISIONS

34-1.
Claims and Penalties

a. MATCH PLAY

In match play if a claim is lodged with the Committee under Rule 2-5, a decision should be given as soon as possible so that the state of the match may, if necessary, be adjusted.

If a claim is not made within the time limit provided by Rule 2-5, it shall not be considered unless it is based on facts previously unknown to the player making the claim and the player making the claim had been given wrong information (Rules 6-2a and 9) by an opponent. In any case, no later claim shall be considered after the result of the match has been officially announced, unless the Committee is satisfied that the opponent knew he was giving wrong information.

b. STROKE PLAY

In stroke play no penalty shall be rescinded, modified or imposed after the competition has closed, except that a penalty of disqualification shall be imposed at any time after the competition has closed if a competitor:

(i) returned a score for any hole lower than actually taken (Rule 6-6d) for any reason other than failure to include a penalty which he did not know he had incurred; or

(ii) returned a score card on which he had recorded a handicap which he knew was higher than that to which he was entitled, and this affected the number of strokes received (Rule 6-2b); or

(iii) was in breach of Rule 1-3.

A competition is deemed to have closed when the result has been officially announced or, in stroke play qualifying followed by match play, when the player has teed off in his first match.

34-2.
Referee's Decision

If a referee has been appointed by the Committee, his decision shall be final.

In the absence of a referee, any dispute or doubtful point on the Rules shall be referred to the Committee, whose decision shall be final.

If the Committee cannot come to a decision, it shall refer the dispute or doubtful point to the Rules of Golf Committee of the United States Golf Association, whose decision shall be final.

If the dispute or doubtful point has not been referred to the Rules of Golf Committee, the player or players have the right to refer an agreed statement through the Secretary of the Club to the Rules of Golf Committee for an opinion as to the correctness of the decision given. The reply will be sent to the Secretary of the Club or Clubs concerned.

If play is conducted other than in accordance with the Rules of Golf, the Rules of Golf Committee will not give a decision on any question.

34-3.
Committee's Decision

Rule 34 deals with the sensitive areas of doubts and disagreements and how to settle them. Each of its provisions deserves careful review:

34-1. Claims and Penalties

Focus on the words "claim" and "wrong information."

A claim boils down to telling your opponent that you think he violated a Rule. In order to be valid, a claim must be timely. It's no good seeing the opponent ground his wedge in a bunker on the ninth hole and bringing it up when you're 1 down playing 18. The statute of limitations for the ninth hole expired when one of you drove from the 10th tee, *since you were aware of the violation.*

Ah, but suppose you didn't know of the violation but it comes to your attention later. In that case, you can claim the hole retroactively on the grounds that your opponent gave you wrong information (even though he gave you no information at all).

Here are some landmark decisions on claims:

• A drives into the rough and finds what he thinks is his ball. He wins the hole. But after his drive on the next hole a player in another match comes up, questions whether or not A played the right ball and, on inspection, A indeed learns that he played the wrong ball. Could B claim the previous hole retroactively? You bet. A gave wrong information.

• There is a deadline for filing a belated claim based on wrong information. That's when the result of a match is officially announced which, in club play, means when the winner's name is posted on a score sheet.

• The level of ethical behavior on the PGA Tour is very high, as illustrated by the incident when Hale Irwin tried to "turn himself in" after a tournament was over. Hale read an account of a penalty applied to another player for dropping in a wrong place, realized he had made the same error, and called the Tour office, saying he was going to return his prize money check of $7,375. The Tour, quite properly under the Rules, refused to accept the check because Hale did not know he had violated a Rule *and* the results of the competition had been announced. If Hale learned of his violation *between* rounds, then the Committee would have had no choice but to disqualify Irwin.

34-2. Referee's Decision

The only time I play with a referee is at a U.S. Open or British Open Championship where it has become the custom to assign a referee to every group of players throughout the championship. It's a neat way to play because it gives us instant access to rulings and, when a ruling is made, one doesn't have to worry about the correctness of the ruling because the referee is the Committee's designated person. Even if he's wrong, he's right—if you take my drift.

In all other events, we play with representatives of the Committee sprinkled around the course ready to help when needed.

34-3. Committee's Decision

Dozens of times every year, written replies to Rules questions from the USGA begin with the ominous words: "The Committee's decision was wrong. However, it was final under Rule 34-3."
It has to be that way. Someone has to be in charge and that someone is inevitably going to make a mistake if he or she works at enough tournaments.

Of course, 99 percent of golf is played informally, and most of that 99 percent is played at match play. If there is a doubt or dispute about the Rules out on the course, the players should try to agree on the facts and then continue on with the match, even though they will not then be certain of the status of the match. They should get a decision from a representative of the Committee (usually the club pro) as soon as possible without delaying play.

Appendix I
LOCAL RULES; CONDITIONS OF THE COMPETITION

LOCAL RULES

Rule 33-8 provides:

"The Committee may make and publish Local Rules for abnormal conditions if they are consistent with the policy of the Governing Authority for the country concerned as set forth in Appendix I to these Rules.

"A penalty imposed by a Rule of Golf shall not be waived by a Local Rule."

Information regarding acceptable and prohibited Local Rules is provided in the *Decisions on the Rules of Golf* under Rule 33-8. Among the matters for which Local Rules may be advisable are the following:

1. Obstructions

Clarifying the status of objects which may be obstructions (Rule 24).

Declaring any construction to be an integral part of the course and, accordingly, not an obstruction, e.g., built-up sides of teeing grounds, putting greens and bunkers (Rules 24 and 33-2a).

2. Roads and Paths

Providing relief of the type afforded under Rule 24-2b from roads and paths not having artificial surfaces and sides if they could unfairly affect play.

3. Preservation of Course

Preservation of the course by defining areas, including turf nurseries and other parts of the course under cultivation, as ground under repair from which play is prohibited.

4. Water Hazards

Lateral Water Hazards. Clarifying the status of sections of water hazards which may be lateral water hazards (Rule 26).

Provisional Ball. Permitting play of a provisional ball for a ball which may be in a water hazard of such character that it would be impracticable to determine whether the ball is in the hazard or to do so would unduly delay play. In such case, if a provisional ball is played and the original ball is in a water hazard, the player may play the original ball as it lies or continue the provisional ball in play, but he may not proceed under Rule 26-1.

5. Defining Bounds and Margins

Specifying means used to define out of bounds, hazards, water hazards, lateral water hazards and ground under repair.

6. Ball Drops

Establishment of special areas on which balls may be dropped when it is not feasible or practicable to proceed exactly in conformity with Rule 24-2b (immovable obstructions), Rule 25-1b or -1c (ground under repair), Rule 26-1 (water hazards and lateral water hazards) and Rule 28 (ball unplayable).

7. Temporary Conditions—Mud, Extreme Wetness

Temporary conditions which might interfere with proper playing of the game, including mud and extreme wetness warranting lifting an embedded ball anywhere through the green (see detailed recommendation below) or removal of mud from a ball through the green.

It's a fundamental duty of any Committee running a competition, or in charge of a course for everyday play, to consider which, if any, of these Local Rules it wishes to install and to make these known to the player. If any of these Local Rules are used day in and day out, they should appear on the back of the course scorecard. When Local Rules are used only for a particular event, or on selected days, they should be posted prominently where players almost *have* to see them, e.g., at the first tee.

Note that Committees are limited to using those Local Rules "consistent with the policy" of the USGA. That is to say, if a Committee installs an alien Local Rule—say one allowing for the repair of spike marks—it has exceeded its authority and has simply walked away from the Rules of Golf.

Following are the suggested texts for other Local Rules that are authorized by the USGA:

Lifting an Embedded Ball

Rule 25-2 provides relief without penalty for a ball embedded in its own pitch-mark in any closely mown area through the green.

On the putting green, a ball may be lifted and damage caused by the impact of a ball may be repaired (Rules 16-1b and c).

When permission to lift an embedded ball anywhere through the green would be warranted, the following Local Rule is suggested:

Anywhere "through the green," a ball which is embedded in its own pitch-mark in the ground, except in loose sand, may be lifted without penalty, cleaned and dropped as near as possible to the spot where it lay but not nearer the hole. (See Rule 20.)
("Through the green" is the whole area of the course except:
a. Teeing ground and putting green of the hole being played;
b. All hazards on the course.)

Exception: A player may not obtain relief under this Rule if it is clearly unreasonable for him to play a stroke because of interference by anything other than the condition covered by this Rule.

Giving relief from embedded balls is now so common that many golfers mistakenly think this relief procedure is automatic. Not so. Relief from embedded balls in any closely mown area (fairways and the aprons of greens) is built right into the structure of the Rules. But if that relief is to be expanded to the rough, a Local Rule needs to say so by granting the right to lift an embedded ball without penalty "through the green."

Practice Between Holes

When, between the play of two holes, it is desired to prohibit practice putting or chipping on or near the putting green of the hole last played, the following Local Rule is recommended:

Between the play of two holes, a player shall not play any practice stroke on or near the putting green of the hole last played. (For other practice, see Rules 7 and 33-2c.)

PENALTY FOR BREACH OF LOCAL RULE:
Match play—Loss of next hole; Stroke play—Two strokes at next hole.

Here is a Local Rule crafted primarily to prohibit the damage that would occur around the hole if every player in a large-field event were to practice putting after completion of a hole. We use it every week on the Tour, but it is not normally used in club events.

Marking Position of Lifted Ball

When it is desired to require a specific means of marking the position of a lifted ball on the putting green, the following Local Rule is recommended:
    Before a ball on the putting green is lifted, its position shall be marked by placing a small coin or some similar object immediately behind the ball; if the ball-marker interferes with another player, it should be moved one or more putterhead-lengths to one side. If the position of the ball is not so marked, *the player shall incur a penalty of one stroke* and the ball shall be replaced. If the ball is not replaced, *the player shall incur the penalty* for breach of Rule 20-3a, but no additional penalty under this Local Rule shall be applied. (This modifies Rule 20-1.)

Another Local Rule that is found useful on the highest levels of competitive golf. I do not recommend its adoption elsewhere.

Prohibition Against Touching Line of Putt with Club

When it is desired to prohibit touching the line of putt with a club in moving loose impediments, the following Local Rule is recommended:
    The line of putt shall not be touched with a club for any purpose except to repair old hole plugs or ball marks or during address. (This modifies Rule 16-1a.)

PENALTY FOR BREACH OF LOCAL RULE:
Match play—Loss of hole; Stroke play—Two strokes.

Again, this is a Local Rule the USGA approved many years ago at the behest of the PGA Tour where it is in effect constantly. Don't give it a second thought unless you are on the verge of becoming a Tour player.

Protection of Young Trees

When it is desired to prevent damage to young trees, the following Local Rule is recommended:
    Protection of young trees identified by_____ — If such a tree interferes with a player's stance or the area of his intended swing, the ball must be lifted, without penalty, and dropped in accordance with the procedure prescribed in Rule 24-2b(i) (Immovable Obstruction).
    The ball may be cleaned when so lifted.

The language of this Local Rule requires that there be a drop without penalty away from young trees (or shrubs) that might expire if slashed with a wedge. Similar language is also acceptable for turf nurseries and flower beds.

Temporary Obstructions

When temporary obstructions are installed for a competition, the following Local Rule is recommended:

1. Definition

Temporary immovable obstructions include tents, scoreboards, grandstands, refreshment stands and lavatories. Any temporary equipment for photography, press, radio and television is also a temporary immovable obstruction, provided it is not mobile or otherwise readily movable.

Excluded are temporary power lines and cables and mats covering them and temporary telephone lines and stanchions supporting them (from which relief is provided in Clause 5) and mobile or otherwise readily movable equipment for photography, press, radio or television (from which relief is obtainable under Rule 24-1).

2. Interference

Interference by a temporary immovable obstruction occurs when (a) the ball lies in or on the obstruction or so close to the obstruction that the obstruction interferes with the player's stance or the area of his intended swing or (b) the obstruction intervenes between the player's ball and the hole or the ball lies within one club-length of a spot where such intervention would exist.

3. Relief

A player may obtain relief from interference by a temporary immovable obstruction as follows:

a. THROUGH THE GREEN
Through the green, the point on the course nearest to where the ball lies shall be determined which (a) is not nearer the hole, (b) avoids interference as defined in Clause 2 of this Local Rule and (c) is not in a hazard or on a putting green. He shall lift the ball and drop it without penalty within one club-length of the point thus determined on ground which fulfills (a), (b) and (c) above.
The ball may be cleaned when so lifted.

b. IN A HAZARD
If the ball lies in a hazard, the player shall lift and drop the ball either:
(i) in the hazard, without penalty, on the nearest ground affording complete relief within the limits specified in Clause 3a above or, if complete relief is impossible, on ground within the hazard affording maximum relief, or
(ii) outside the hazard, *under penalty of one stroke,* as follows: The player shall determine the point on the course nearest to where the ball lies which (a) is not nearer the hole, (b) avoids interference as defined in Clause 2 of this Local Rule and (c) is not in a hazard. He shall drop the ball within one club-length of the point thus determined on ground which fulfills (a), (b) and (c) above.

The ball may be cleaned when so lifted.

Exception: A player may not obtain relief from a temporary immovable obstruction under Clause 3a or 3b if (a) it is clearly unreasonable for him to play a stroke, or in the case of intervention to play a stroke directly toward the obstruction, because of interference by anything other than the obstruction or (b) interference would occur only through use of an unnecessarily abnormal stance, swing or direction of play.

4. Ball Lost in Temporary Immovable Obstruction
If there is reasonable evidence that a ball is lost within the confines of a temporary immovable obstruction, the player may take relief without penalty as prescribed in Rule 24-2c.

5. Temporary Power Lines and Cables
The above Clauses do not apply to (1) temporary power lines or cables or mats covering them or (2) temporary telephone lines or stanchions supporting them. If such items are readily movable, the player may obtain relief under Rule 24-1. If they are not readily movable, the player may, if the ball lies through the green, obtain relief as provided in Rule 24-2b(i). If the ball lies in a bunker or a water hazard, the player may obtain relief under Rule 24-2b(i), except that the ball must be dropped in the bunker or water hazard.

Note: *The prohibition in Rule 24-2b(i) against crossing over, through or under the obstruction does not apply.*

If a ball strikes a temporary power line or cable which is elevated, it must be replayed, without penalty (see Rule 20-5). If the ball is not immediately recoverable, another ball may be substituted.

Exception: Ball striking elevated junction section of cable rising from the ground shall not be replayed.

6. Re-Dropping
If a dropped ball rolls into a position covered by this Local Rule, or nearer the hole than its original position, it shall be re-dropped without penalty. If it again rolls into such a position, it shall be placed where it first struck a part of the course when re-dropped.

PENALTY FOR BREACH OF LOCAL RULE:
Match play—Loss of hole; Stroke play—Two strokes.

This was the language necessary for dealing with the accouterments of modern big-time golf where there is a consensus that line-of-sight relief should be afforded for things like scoreboards and grandstands. An understanding of the procedure might add to the television viewer's experience, but it is otherwise of no practical consequence to recreational golfers.

**"Preferred Lies"
and "Winter Rules"**

The USGA does not endorse "preferred lies" and "winter rules" and recommends that the Rules of Golf be observed uniformly. Ground under repair is provided for in Rule 25. Occasional abnormal conditions which might interfere with fair play and are not widespread should be defined accurately as ground under repair.

However, adverse conditions are sometimes so general throughout a course that the Committee believes "preferred lies" or "winter rules" would promote fair play or help protect the course. Heavy snows, spring thaws, prolonged rains or extreme heat can make fairways unsatisfactory and sometimes prevent use of heavy mowing equipment.

When a Committee adopts a Local Rule for "preferred lies" or "winter rules," it should be in detail and should be interpreted by the Committee, as there is no established code for "winter rules." Without a detailed Local Rule, it is meaningless for a Committee to post a notice merely saying "Winter Rules Today."

The following Local Rule would seem appropriate for the conditions in question, but the USGA will not interpret it:

A ball lying on a "fairway" may be lifted and cleaned, without penalty, and placed within one club-length of where it originally lay, not nearer the hole, and so as to preserve as nearly as possible the stance required to play from the original lie. A ball so lifted is back in play when the player addresses it or, if he does not address it, when he makes his next stroke at it.

Before a Committee adopts a Local Rule permitting "preferred lies" or "winter rules," the following facts should be considered:

1. Such a Local Rule conflicts with the Rules of Golf and the fundamental principle of playing the ball as it lies.

2. "Winter rules" are sometimes adopted under the guise of protecting the course when, in fact, the practical effect is just the opposite—they permit moving the ball to the best turf, from which divots are then taken to injure the course further.

3. "Preferred lies" or "winter rules" tend generally to lower scores and handicaps, thus penalizing the players in competition with players whose scores for handicaps are made under the Rules of Golf.

4. Extended use or indiscriminate use of "preferred lies" or "winter rules" will place players at a disadvantage when competing at a course where the ball must be played as it lies.

Handicapping and "Preferred Lies"

Scores made under a Local Rule for "preferred lies" or "winter rules" may be accepted for handicapping if the Committee considers that conditions warrant.

When such a Local Rule is adopted, the Committee should ensure that the course's normal scoring difficulty is maintained as nearly as possible through adjustment of tee-markers and related methods. However, if extreme conditions cause extended use of "preferred lies" or "winter rules" and the course management cannot adjust scoring difficulty properly, the club should obtain a Temporary Course Rating from its district golf association.

Main point: It's no good posting a sign that reads "Winter Rules in Effect" because that notice doesn't tell a golfer anything other than he's going to be able to do otherwise than play the ball as it lies. But where? And does he drop or place it? And when is the ball in play? The language that the USGA deems "appropriate" in this Local Rule answers all those questions.

CONDITIONS OF THE COMPETITION

Rule 33-1 states: "The Committee shall lay down the conditions under which a competition is to be played." Conditions should include such matters as method of entry, eligibility requirements, format, the method of deciding ties, the method of determining the draw for match play and handicap allowances for a handicap competition.

Rule 33-6 empowers the Committee to determine how and when a halved match or a stroke play tie shall be decided. The decision should be published in advance.
The USGA recommends:

How to Decide Ties

1. Match Play
A match which ends all square should be played off hole by hole until one side wins a hole. The play-off should start on the hole where the match began. In a handicap match, handicap strokes should be allowed as in the prescribed round.

2. Stroke Play
(a) In the event of a tie in a scratch stroke play competition, an 18-hole play-off is recommended. If that is not feasible, a hole-by-hole play-off is recommended.

(b) In the event of a tie in a handicap stroke play competition, a play-off over 18 holes with handicaps is recommended. If a shorter play-off is necessary, the percentage of 18 holes to be played should be applied to the players' handicaps to determine their play-off handicaps. It is advisable to arrange for a percentage of holes that will result in whole numbers in handicaps; if this is not feasible, handicap stroke fractions of one-half stroke or more should count as a full stroke and any lesser fraction should be disregarded.

(c) In either a scratch or handicap stroke play competition, if a play-off of any type is not feasible, matching score cards is recommended. The method of matching cards should be announced in advance. An acceptable method of matching cards is to determine the winner on the basis of the best score for the last nine holes. If the tying players have the same score for the last nine, determine the winner on the basis of the last six holes, last three holes and finally the 18th hole. If such a method is used in a handicap stroke play competition, one-half, one-third, one-sixth, etc., of the handicaps should be deducted.

(d) If the conditions of the competition provide that ties shall be decided over the last nine, last six, last three and last hole, they should also provide what will happen if this procedure does not produce a winner.

Note that these methods of resolving ties are USGA recommendations. They may not be practical or desirable for every event. That doesn't matter. What matters is that the tie-breaker be determined and announced in advance. Making that determination after the fact is sure to incense somebody.

Draw for Match Play

Although the draw for match play may be completely blind or certain players may be distributed through different quarters or eighths, the General Numerical Draw is recommended if flights are determined by a qualifying round.

General Numerical Draw

For purposes of determining places in the draw, ties in qualifying rounds other than those for the last qualifying place shall be decided by the order in which scores are returned, the first score to be returned receiving the lowest available number, etc. If it is impossible to determine the order in which scores are returned, ties shall be determined by a blind draw.

UPPER HALF	LOWER HALF	UPPER HALF	LOWER HALF
64 QUALIFIERS		32 QUALIFIERS	
1 vs. 64	2 vs. 63	1 vs. 32	2 vs. 31
32 vs. 33	31 vs. 34	16 vs. 17	15 vs. 18
16 vs. 49	15 vs. 50	8 vs. 25	7 vs. 26
17 vs. 48	18 vs. 47	9 vs. 24	10 vs. 23
8 vs. 57	7 vs. 58	4 vs. 29	3 vs. 30
25 vs. 40	26 vs. 39	13 vs. 20	14 vs. 19
9 vs. 56	10 vs. 55	5 vs. 28	6 vs. 27
24 vs. 41	23 vs. 42	12 vs. 21	11 vs. 22
4 vs. 61	3 vs. 62	16 QUALIFIERS	
29 vs. 36	30 vs. 35	1 vs. 16	2 vs. 15
13 vs. 52	14 vs. 51	8 vs. 9	7 vs. 10
20 vs. 45	19 vs. 46	4 vs. 13	3 vs. 14
5 vs. 60	6 vs. 59	5 vs. 12	6 vs. 11
28 vs. 37	27 vs. 38	8 QUALIFIERS	
12 vs. 53	11 vs. 54	1 vs. 8	2 vs. 7
21 vs. 44	22 vs. 43	4 vs. 5	3 vs. 6

The USGA recommends the following handicap allowances in handicap competitions:

Singles match play: Allow the higher-handicapped player the full difference between the handicaps of the two players.

Four-ball match play: Reduce the handicaps of all four players by the handicap of the low-handicapped player, who shall then play from scratch. Allow each of the three other players 100 percent of the resulting difference.

Individual stroke play: Allow the full handicap.

Four-ball stroke play: Men—Allow each competitor 90 percent of his handicap. Women—Allow each competitor 95 percent of her handicap.

Best-ball-of-four, stroke play: Men—Allow each competitor 80 percent of his handicap. Women—Allow each competitor 90 percent of her handicap.

Again, these are labeled as recommendations rather than as USGA "musts," but I urge that they be accepted. The USGA Handicap Committee has worked these out in an attempt to come up with a level playing field in the various kinds of handicap competitions.

The following are some conditions which a Committee may wish to make:

List of Conforming Golf Balls

The USGA periodically issues a List of Conforming Golf Balls. If it is desired to require use of a brand of golf ball on the List, the List should be posted and the following issued as a condition of the competition:

> Only brands of golf balls on the USGA's latest List of Conforming Golf Balls may be used. Penalty for use of brand not on the List: Disqualification.

This is a supercautious "condition" advanced with the suspicion that there might be some kind of juiced-up ball out there that has not been tested by the USGA. It is used in USGA championships and on the Tour, but don't give it a second thought.

One-Ball Rule

If it is desired to prohibit changing brands of golf balls during a stipulated round, the following condition is recommended; it is suggested that it be considered only for competitions involving expert players:

Limitation on Golf Balls Used During Round
(Condition: Rules 5-1 and 33-1)

1. BALLS WITH IDENTICAL MARKINGS TO BE USED

Throughout a stipulated round, the player is limited to golf balls with identical markings, except that the player-identification numbers may differ by number only, not by color.

153

PENALTY FOR BREACH OF CONDITION:

Match play—At the conclusion of the hole at which the breach is discovered, the state of the match shall be adjusted by deducting one hole for each hole at which a breach occurred. Maximum deduction per round: two holes.

Stroke play—Two strokes for each hole at which any breach occurred; maximum penalty per round: four strokes.

2. PROCEDURE WHEN BREACH DISCOVERED:

When a player discovers that he has used a ball in breach of this condition, he shall abandon that ball before playing from the next teeing ground and complete the round using a proper ball; otherwise, *the player shall be disqualified.* If discovery is made during play of a hole and the player elects to substitute a proper ball before completing that hole, the player shall place a proper ball on the spot where the ball used in breach of this condition lay.

This is a Condition, the adoption of which was urged by myself and others who were concerned in the 1970s when some players began trying to select a ball, rather than use their skills, to shape a shot. For example, there seemed to be preferable balls to play into the wind, or downwind. The one-ball rule put a stop to that. But its introduction into club golf would be both unnecessary and a nuisance.

Time of Starting

If the Committee desires to adopt the condition in the Note under Rule 6-3a, the following wording is recommended:

Rule 6-3a provides: "The player shall start at the time laid down by the Committee." The penalty for breach of Rule 6-3a is disqualification. However, it is a condition of the competition that, if the player arrives at his starting point, ready to play, within five minutes after his starting time, in the absence of circumstances which warrant waiving the penalty of disqualification as provided in Rule 33-7, the penalty for failure to start on time is loss of the first hole in match play or two strokes at the first hole in stroke play instead of disqualification.

Here's a Condition I think clubs would be wise to install. The penalty, under the Rule, for showing up late, even a minute late, is disqualification. But in this Condition the DQ is scaled down to loss of the first hole in a match or two strokes in stroke play if the lateness is under five minutes.

Practice

The Committee may make regulations governing practice in accordance with the Note to Rule 7-1, Clause (c) of the Exception under Rule 7-2 and Rule 33-2c.

Advice in Team Competitions

If the Committee desires to adopt the condition in the Note under

Rule 8, which applies to a team competition with or without concurrent individual competition, the following wording is recommended:

In accordance with the Note to Rule 8 of the Rules of Golf, each team may appoint one person (in addition to the persons from whom advice may be asked under Rule 8-1) who may give advice (including pointing out a line for putting) to members of that team. Such person [if it is desired to put a restriction on who may be appointed, insert such restriction here] shall be identified to the Committee prior to the start of the competition.

Automotive Transportation

If it is desired to prohibit automotive transportation in a competition, the following condition is suggested:

Players shall not use automotive transportation during play.

PENALTY FOR BREACH OF CONDITION:

Match play—At the conclusion of the hole at which the breach is discovered, the state of the match shall be adjusted by deducting one hole for each hole at which a breach occurred. Maximum deduction per round: two holes.

Stroke play—Two strokes for each hole at which any breach occurred; maximum penalty per round: four strokes.

Match or stroke play—Use of any unauthorized automotive vehicle shall be discontinued immediately upon discovery that a breach has occurred. Otherwise, the player shall be disqualified.

The thought to carry away from this Condition is that it's OK to ride in a cart *unless* the Committee says otherwise.

RULES QUIZ

So now you know it all! You've plowed through my admonitions on Etiquette, the Definitions, the 34 Rules and Appendix I.

I hope you have enjoyed your labors and have profited from them. For your final exam I have included a quiz primarily devised by Tom Meeks, USGA Director of Rules and Competitions, to test the knowledge of students at a Rules of Golf workshop. It's meant to test your ability to *use* this book rather than your ability to snap off the correct answers. It's very much an open-book test, and each and every answer is readily available within the Rules proper.

The best way to join in the challenge of this quiz is to try to answer as many questions as possible within 30 minutes.

It is not intended to be an easy quiz. Anything but! If you can answer 40 of the 50 questions correctly within the 30 minutes, you're not far from being an expert. Anything better than that and you are one already! Good luck, and thanks for being an interested student.

The answers to the quiz appear on page 170.

1. Which of the following is not a loose impediment?

_____a. Leaves.

_____b. Dew.

_____c. Stones.

_____d. Twigs.

2. The line of putt may be touched except:

_____a. To remove loose impediments on the putting green.

_____b. To repair old hole plugs on the putting green.

_____c. To tap down spike marks on the putting green.

_____d. To repair ball marks on the putting green.

3. In match play, if a player plays when his opponent should have played:

_____a. The player loses the hole.

_____b. No penalty is incurred and the ball shall be played as it lies.

_____c. The player incurs a one-stroke penalty and the ball shall be played as it lies.

_____d. The opponent may immediately require the player to cancel the stroke so played and play a ball in correct order, without penalty.

4. A ball embedded in its own pitch-mark in the ground in any closely mown area through the green may be:

_____a. Lifted, cleaned and dropped, without penalty, within one club-length of the spot where it lay but not nearer the hole.

_____b. Lifted, cleaned and placed, without penalty, within one club-length of the spot where it lay but not nearer the hole.

_____c. Lifted, cleaned and placed, without penalty, as near as possible to the spot where it lay but not nearer the hole.

_____d. Lifted, cleaned and dropped, without penalty, as near as possible to the spot where it lay but not nearer the hole.

5. Which of the following would be considered a breach of Rule 8-1, Advice?

_____a. A player's caddie takes one of his clubs and swings it to show him how to play a certain shot.

_____b. After 18 holes in a 36-hole match, a player asks his golf professional for help with his putting.

_____c. A player removes a towel covering another player's clubs to determine which club was used for his last stroke.

_____d. A player looks into another player's golf bag to determine which club was used for his last stroke.

6. Which one of the following statements is false?

_____a. In searching for his ball anywhere on the course, the player may touch or bend long grass, but only to the extent necessary to find and identify it, provided that this does not improve the lie of the ball, the area of his intended swing or his line of play.

_____b. A player is entitled to see his ball when playing a stroke.

_____c. In a hazard, if a ball is covered by loose impediments or sand, the player may remove by probing, raking or other means as much thereof as will enable him to see a part of the ball.

_____d. If a ball is believed to be lying in water in a water hazard, the player may probe for it with a club or otherwise.

7. Which of the following statements is false?

_____a. The player's ball shall not strike the flagstick when attended, removed or held up by the player, his partner or either of their caddies.

_____b. The player's ball shall not strike the flagstick in the hole, unattended, when the ball has been played from a greenside bunker.

_____c. The player's ball shall not strike the flagstick in the hole, unattended, when the ball has been played from the putting green.

_____d. The player's ball shall not strike the player's caddie, his partner, or his partner's caddie when attending the flagstick.

8. Which one of the following statements is false?

_____a. When out of bounds is defined by a line on the ground, the line itself is out of bounds.

_____b. A player may not stand out of bounds to play a ball lying within bounds.

_____c. A ball is out of bounds when all of it lies out of bounds.

_____d. The out-of-bounds line extends vertically upwards and downwards.

9. When a player's ball lies in a bunker, he may do which of the following:

_____a. Ground his club.

___×___b. Remove a loose stone behind the ball.

_____c. Place his clubs in the bunker.

_____d. Smooth footprints anywhere in the bunker.

10. Which of the following is true?

___✓___a. A player who begins a round with thirteen clubs may add a club to bring the total to fourteen.

_____b. A player, starting a round with fourteen clubs, breaks his putter in anger after missing a short putt. He is entitled to replace it without penalty.

_____c. A player, starting a round with fourteen clubs, loses his putter during the round. He is entitled to replace the lost putter with another putter without penalty.

_____d. Before the start of a round, a player, realizing he has fifteen clubs in his bag, declares one club out of play, removes it from his bag and places it on the floor of his golf cart. He incurs no penalty.

11. A player may declare his ball unplayable:

___No__a. Only if his opponent agrees that the ball is unplayable.

___No__b. Only in a bunker.

___No__c. In a water hazard.

_____d. Anywhere on the course, except in a water hazard.

12. A "foursome" is:

_____a. A group of four players.

_____b. A match where all four players are playing individual matches against each other.

___✓___c. A match in which two play against two and each side plays one ball.

_____d. A match in which two play their better ball against the better ball of the two other players.

13. In which of the following cases must a player play his dropped ball as it lies when taking relief from a lateral water hazard?

_____a. If the ball rolls back into the lateral water hazard.

161

_____b. If the ball rolls onto the putting green.

_____c. If the ball rolls and comes to rest outside the lateral water hazard but into a position where the player must stand in the hazard to play the stroke.

_____d. If the ball rolls into a bunker which is less than two club-lengths from the lateral water hazard.

14. In match play, a player and his opponent exchange balls during the play of a hole, but they cannot determine who played the wrong ball first. What is the proper procedure?

_____a. The hole should be considered halved.

_____b. The players should replay the hole.

_____c. The players should play out the hole with the balls exchanged.

_____d. Both players are disqualified.

15. Which of the following is automatically considered ground under repair?

_____a. A pile of grass cuttings that has been piled up for removal.

_____b. A bad area in the fairway.

_____c. A pile of cut logs and branches that have been lying in a remote area for years.

_____d. A flower bed on the course.

16. A player hits a ball into casual water and cannot find it. What is the proper procedure?

_____a. The player must treat it as a lost ball and proceed under the stroke and distance penalty.

_____b. The player incurs a one-stroke penalty and must drop a ball as near as possible to where the ball last entered the casual water.

_____c. There is no penalty and the player shall drop a ball within one club-length of the point nearest to where the ball last crossed the margin of the casual water which is (1) not nearer the hole than where it last crossed the margin of the casual water, (2) avoids interference by the casual water and (3) is not in a hazard or on a putting green.

_____d. There is no such thing as a ball lost in casual water in the Rules of Golf.

17. A ball comes to rest in an area which is on the course, but near out of bounds. A brick patio which is located out of bounds interferes with the player's swing. What is the proper procedure?

_____a. The player is not entitled to relief from the brick patio because immovable artificial objects off the course are not obstructions.

_____b. The player is entitled to relief and may drop a ball within one club-length of the point which avoids interference, no closer to the hole.

_____c. The player is entitled to relief and, under penalty of one stroke, may drop a ball within one club-length of the point which avoids interference, no closer to the hole.

_____d. The player is entitled to relief only if the ball lies out of bounds.

18. A "teeing ground" is correctly defined as which of the following?

_____a. Any part of the mown area identified by markers.

_____b. A rectangular area two-club lengths in depth, the front and sides of which are defined by the outside limits of the tee-markers.

_____c. A rectangular area one club-length in depth, the front and sides of which are defined by the outside limits of the tee-markers.

_____d. A rectangular area, the front and sides of which are defined by the outside limits of the tee-markers. There is no limit to the depth of the teeing ground.

19. In which of the following circumstances is a player penalized for causing his ball to move?

_____a. In measuring to determine which ball is farther from the hole.

_____b. In removing a movable obstruction.

_____c. In searching for a ball in a bunker.

_____d. In removing a loose impediment within a club-length of the ball.

20. In which of the following circumstances is a player prohibited from cleaning his ball?

_____a. In taking relief from ground under repair.

_____b. In lifting his ball to determine if it is unfit for play.

_____c. In taking relief from an immovable obstruction.

_____d. In lifting a ball on the putting green.

21. Which of the following statements is true?

_____a. In stroke play, a competitor can concede a fellow-competitor's next stroke.

_____b. A player can repair spike marks on his line of putt at any time.

_____c. In four-ball stroke play, both the competitor and his partner must sign their scorecard.

_____d. A player may not play a second ball under Rule 3-3 in match play.

163

22. Which of the following is false?

        ×   a. In match play, play of a provisional ball is prohibited.

        ×   b. The Committee is responsible for adding the score cards.

            c. A player can declare his ball unplayable anywhere on the course, except in a water hazard.

            d. A player can start a round with no more than fourteen clubs.

23. A player's ball comes to rest on a bridge in a water hazard. What are the player's options?

            a. The player may play the ball as it lies, but he cannot ground his club on the bridge.

            b. The player is entitled to relief without penalty because the bridge is an immovable obstruction.

       ✓   c. The player may play the ball as it lies and ground his club or he may proceed, under penalty of one stroke, under the water hazard Rule (26-1).

            d. The player must proceed under the water hazard Rule (26-1), under penalty of one stroke.

24. In a match, player A, who has already holed out in four, concedes his opponent's (B) next stroke which was a two-foot putt for a 4. B declines A's concession and misses the putt. What is the result of the hole?

            a. Player A wins the hole because player B putted out after his putt for 4 was conceded.

       ✓   b. The hole was halved. A concession cannot be declined or withdrawn.

            c. Player A wins the hole because B was within his rights to decline A's concession and he subsequently missed the putt for a halve.

            d. Player A loses the hole because an opponent's next stroke cannot be conceded in match play.

25. A competitor plays from outside the teeing ground on the ninth hole and scores a 5. He then plays from the 10th tee before realizing his error. What is the ruling?

            a. The competitor is penalized two strokes and scores a 7 for the ninth hole.

            b. The competitor is penalized one stroke and scores a 6 for the ninth hole.

            c. The competitor must replay the ninth hole and add the two-stroke penalty.

            d. The competitor is disqualified.

26. A competitor taps in a one-foot putt for a 3 with the handle of his putter. What is his score for the hole?

_____a. No penalty - 3 and the ball is holed.

_____b. One-stroke penalty - 4 and the ball is holed.

_____c. Two-stroke penalty - 5 and the ball is holed.

_____d. No penalty, but he must cancel the stroke and replay it using the clubhead.

27. In which of the following situations is a player not penalized when his ball in play moves?

_____a. The player's caddie accidentally moves the player's ball during search.

_____b. After the player has addressed the ball.

_____c. In the course of a practice swing the player's club accidentally strikes the ball.

_____d. The player's opponent accidentally kicks the player's ball during search.

28. A player must re-drop a ball without penalty:

_____a. If it rolls out of bounds.

_____b. If it rolls onto a putting green.

_____c. If it rolls into a hazard.

_____d. A ball must be re-dropped without penalty in all of the above situations.

29. Which of the following may not be used during a stipulated round?

_____a. A plain glove.

_____b. A handkerchief wrapped around a grip.

_____c. A compass.

_____d. Binoculars without a range-finder.

30. In stroke play, a player's ball deflects off a tree and hits his caddie. The ball comes to rest in a very bad lie. What is the ruling?

_____a. There is no penalty because the player's caddie is an outside agency.

_____b. The player incurs a one-stroke penalty and must play the ball as it lies.

_____c. The player incurs a two-stroke penalty and must replay the stroke.

_____d. The player incurs a two-stroke penalty and must play the ball as it lies.

31. A ball is unfit for play if:

_____a. Mud adheres to it.

___x___b. It is visibly cracked.

_____c. Its paint is discolored.

___x___d. Its surface is scratched or scraped.

32. In stroke play, a competitor returns his score card to the Committee. The hole-by-hole scores are correct, but the competitor records a total score which is one stroke lower than his actual total score. What is the ruling?

_____a. The competitor is disqualified for returning an incorrect score card.

___✓___b. There is no penalty to the competitor because he is only responsible for the correctness of the hole-by-hole scores. The Committee is responsible for the addition of scores.

_____c. Both the competitor and his marker are disqualified for returning an incorrect score card.

_____d. The competitor incurs the general penalty of two strokes for returning an incorrect score card.

33. Which of the following constitutes practice during a round prohibited by Rule 7-2?

_____a. Playing a practice putt on the practice putting green after completing play of the ninth hole while waiting for the group ahead to play from the 10th tee.

_____b. Playing a practice chip from the fringe to the putting green of the hole last played.

___x___c. While waiting to play to the putting green, a player dropped a ball on the fairway and struck it with his putter.

_____d. A player flicks a range ball back toward the driving range with the back of a club while walking down the fairway.

34. A player may lift his ball if he believes it might assist any other player:

_____a. Only if both balls lie on the putting green.

_____b. Only at the request of another player.

___✓___c. At any time, provided another ball is not in motion.

_____d. Only in match play.

35. A movable obstruction may be removed:

_____a. Except when both the ball and the obstruction lie in a hazard.

_____b. Except when the ball is on the course and the obstruction is out of bounds.

_____c. At any time regardless of the location of the obstruction and the ball.

_____d. Only if the ball lies through the green.

36. Which of the following is false?

_____a. In four-ball match play a side may be represented by one partner.

_____b. Partners in a four-ball match can give advice to each other.

_____c. A side can play in the order it considers best.

_____d. A and B are to play C and D in a four-ball match. A and C agree to repair spike marks contrary to Rule 16-1c. Since A and C agreed to waive a Rule of Golf, they are disqualified from the match, but B and D can represent each side and play the match.

37. In which of the following circumstances is the player penalized for moving his ball in play?

_____a. In the process of marking his ball on the putting green.

_____b. In measuring to determine which ball is farther from the hole.

_____c. In the process of removing a loose impediment on the putting green which is a few inches from his ball.

_____d. While searching for his ball during a match.

38. A player's ball at rest through the green is accidentally moved by a maintenance vehicle. The spot where the ball was moved from is not precisely known. What is the proper procedure?

_____a. The ball shall be dropped as near as possible to the place where it lay but not in a hazard.

_____b. The ball must be placed as near as possible to the place where it lay.

_____c. The ball must be dropped within one club-length of where it lay.

_____d. The ball must be played as it lies.

39. A loose impediment on a player's line of putt may be removed:

_____a. By any means.

_____b. Only by picking it up.

_____c. By either picking it up or brushing it aside with his hand or club without pressing anything down.

_____d. A loose impediment on the line of putt cannot be removed.

40. In an individual stroke play competition held at handicap, a player fails to record his handicap on his score card before returning his score card to the Committee. The error is discovered before the competition closes. What is the ruling?

_____a. The player is disqualified.

_____b. The player's handicap for the round is deemed to be zero.

_____c. The player incurs no penalty and can correct the error.

_____d. The player incurs a two-stroke penalty which is added to his score for the first hole.

41. In a match, player A who has holed out in four gives advice to player B, his opponent, who is putting for a 4. What is the ruling?

_____a. The hole is halved.

_____b. Player A incurs a two-stroke penalty and B has two putts to win the hole.

_____c. Player A loses the hole for giving advice.

_____d. There is no penalty and B must putt for the half.

42. Which of the following is false?

_____a. A side is dormie when it is as many holes down as there are left to play.

_____b. The hole is 4¼ inches in diameter.

_____c. A second ball played under Rule 3-3 can only be played in stroke play.

_____d. A player's caddie is not an outside agency.

43. A stroke play competition is deemed to have closed:

_____a. When the winning putt has been holed.

_____b. When the result has been officially announced.

_____c. When the final group has left the putting green of the last hole played.

_____d. At midnight of the last round of the competition.

44. In which of the following cases is a player prohibited from cleaning his ball?

_____a. To determine if it is unfit for play.

_____b. In taking relief from an immovable obstruction.

_____c. In taking relief from casual water.

_____d. In replacing a ball that was moved by an outside agency.

45. Which of the following is not an artificial device?

_____a. A compass.

_____b. A pencil specially marked to gauge distance.

_____c. Audiotapes with instructional information used during a round.

_____d. Binoculars with no range-finder attachments.

46. Which of the following is true?

_____a. An internal boundary is not permitted under the Rules of Golf.

_____b. A and B who are partners may share a maximum of 14 clubs between them.

_____c. A half-eaten apple lying in a bunker is not a loose impediment.

_____d. A competitor incurs a loss-of-hole penalty if he plays a fellow-competitor's ball.

47. Which of the following is a wrong ball?

_____a. A provisional ball.

_____b. A ball substituted for a ball which has been lifted from the putting green.

_____c. A ball played from outside the teeing ground.

_____d. A ball played from out of bounds.

48. In a match, a player lifts his ball to determine if it is unfit for play without announcing his intention in advance to his opponent, without marking the position of the ball and he cleans the ball. What is the penalty?

_____a. The player incurs a one-stroke penalty.

_____b. The player incurs a two-stroke penalty.

_____c. The player incurs three one-stroke penalties for a total penalty of three strokes.

_____d. The player loses the hole.

49. Which of the following is an obstruction?

_____a. Grass clippings piled for removal.

_____b. The player's golf bag.

_____c. A stake defining out of bounds.

_____d. A stake defining a water hazard.

50. A player putts his ball off the putting green and into a bunker. He declares the ball unplayable. Which of the following procedures may he follow under penalty of one stroke?

_____a. Place a ball as nearly as possible at the spot on the putting green from which the original ball was last played.

b. Drop a ball as nearly as possible at the spot on the putting green from which the original ball was last played.

c. Drop a ball outside the bunker within two club-lengths of the spot where the ball entered the bunker.

d. Drop a ball outside the bunker keeping the spot where the ball lay unplayable in the bunker directly between the hole and the spot on which the ball is dropped.

ANSWERS

1. b (Definition—Loose Impediment)	25. d (Rule 11-4)
2. c (Rule 16-1a)	26. c (Rule 14-1)
3. d (Rule 10-4a)	27. d (Rule 18-3a)
4. d (Rule 25-2)	28. d (Rule 20-2c)
5. c (Decision 8-1/11)	29. c (Rule 14-3)
6. b (Rule 12-1)	30. d (Rule 19-2b)
7. b (Rule 17-3)	31. b (Rule 5-3)
8. b (Definition—Out of Bounds)	32. b (Decision 6-6d/2)
9. c (Rule 13-4)	33. c (Decision 7-2/2)
10. a (Rule 4-4a)	34. c (Rule 22)
11. d (Rule 28)	35. c (Rule 24-1)
12. c (Rule 29)	36. d (Rule 30-3e and Rule 1-3)
13. c (Rule 20-2c)	37. d (Rule 18-2a)
14. c (Rule 15-2)	38. a (Rule 18-1 and Rule 20-3c)
15. a (Definition—Ground Under Repair)	39. c (Rule 16-1a(i))
16. c (Rule 25-1c)	40. a (Rule 6-2b)
17. a (Definition—Obstruction)	41. a (Rule 2-2)
18. b (Definition—Teeing Ground)	42. a (Rule 2-1)
19. d (Rule 18-2c)	43. b (Rule 34-1b)
20. b (Rule 21)	44. a (Rule 21)
21. d (Rule 3-3)	45. d (Rule 14-3)
22. a (Rule 27-2)	46. b (Rule 4-4a)
23. c (Rule 13-4 and Rule 24-2)	47. d (Definition of Wrong Ball)
24. b (Rule 2-4)	48. a (Rule 5-3)
	49. d (Definition—Obstruction)
	50. a (Rule 28a)

INDEX